G000090152

THE UPS AND DOWNS OF THE PROPERTY LADDER

What to do when times are tough

www.housingcrunch.co.uk

THE UPS AND DOWNS OF THE PROPERTY LADDER

What to do when times are tough

Andrew Stanway

Stobart Davies

©2009 Andrew Stanway

All rights reserved: No part of this publication may be reproduced, stored in a retrieval system, or transmitted in any form or by any means – electronic, mechanical, photocopying, recording, or otherwise – without prior written permission from the publisher or a licence permitting restricted copying issued by the Copyright Licensing Agency, 90 Tottenham Court Road, London W1P 0LA. This book may not be lent, resold, hired out or otherwise disposed of by trade in any form of binding or cover other than that in which it is published, without the prior consent of the publisher.

Moral rights: The Author has asserted his moral right to be identified as the Author of this Work.

Published: 2009 by Stobart Davies Limited
Stobart House, Pontyclerc
Penybanc Road, Ammanford
Carmarthenshire SA18 3HP, UK
www.stobartdavies.com

British Library Cataloguing in Publication Data
A CIP record for this book is available from the British Library.

ISBN: 978-0-85442-136-7

Typesetting and design by: Stobart Davies Ltd, Ammanford

Front cover design: Agile Marketing, Bradford-on-Avon

Printed by: Bell & Bain Ltd., Glasgow

Disclaimer: The opinions expressed and the material within this book are for general information only and do not constitute investment, tax, legal or other forms of advice. You should not rely on this information to make (or refrain from making) any decisions. Always obtain independent, professional advice for your own particular situation.

CONTENTS

Throughout the book, when I say 'he', as applied to builders, estate agents, surveyors, and so on, I also mean 'she'.

Also, when I talk of 'houses' I mean this to cover flats and every other sort of home.

INTRODUCTION

I have been fascinated by and involved with the property market for more than 40 years. As a psychotherapist for 20 years I was also intrigued by the emotional and psychological aspects of housing and everything that flows from it in people's lives and relationships. Having lived in some 20 homes (both rented and owned, in three countries) over my lifetime, and having worked as a project manager on domestic builds over the last 15 years, I have an experience of the housing market not just from my own perspective but also through the eyes of many of those with whom I have dealt over the years.

Throughout this time there have been all manner of ups and downs in the housing market. Yet I've never been tempted to write about the subject before because it was my belief and experience that prices of houses rise and fall like those of other commodities and that, on balance, the downturns whilst painful for a while, come good in the end. That no one learns much from these changes in an effort to prevent them in the future is perhaps simply a reflection of human nature. Like the teenager on his motorbike, we irrationally believe that disaster is something that happens to others while we somehow live a charmed life and remain immune.

This denial has been just one symptom of our national obsession with our homes…or what most people have come, significantly, to refer to as their 'property', over the last 15 years. Dozens of TV programmes and other media have created a sort of 'property porn', increasing our lust for easy profit and gratification and a hubris that simply had to end. But as with the magazine centrefold, the source of the excitement is only an illusion on paper. We have projected our self-centred greed and fear on to our homes in a way that could only end in tears. We have collectively become a nation of dirty-Mack, dinner-party-bragging self-abusers and are now getting our come-uppance.

This attitude has come about because although, very obviously, our homes are an investment in that we have large sums of money tied up in them, most of us have come to use the term 'investment' in a rather one-sided (win-win) way when applied to the place we live. Because the value of our homes has risen so dramatically over the last 15 years we have lost sight of the fact that it is the very nature of investments to rise *and* fall in value. It has also seduced us into believing that property is *in fact* the only investment worth having. Of course this isn't true, and never has been. I hope that current events in the property and financial markets will make people think again about spreading their investments across several asset classes.

The reason to speak out now is that things are probably far worse than most pundits will admit; and the world in general is a very different place. Never has anyone in this generation seen main-stream banks getting into such trouble (the banks themselves say they have no idea what their true exposure is to recent property-based losses); never before have so many people been living on the financial edge (more than one million UK households say they have savings that will last them for just two weeks at their current rate of expenditure, were they to lose their job); and never before in peacetime have world-wide economic conditions been so challenging. The average British household in is debt for £60,000 and the number of personal insolvencies is rising.

The number of households spending more than a third of their income servicing debt trebled between mid-2007 and mid-2008.

The cost of daily essentials such as food, energy and fuel is also rising, putting ordinary householders under increased pressure, whatever is happening to their homes. The average family's grocery costs have risen by £1,400 in the last year and the cost of filling the tank of a mid-sized car has risen by £10 over the same period. This, added to increased borrowing costs, has left many households feeling financially insecure for the first time for many years. The number of borrowers who have missed three or more mortgage payments has more than doubled, to 300,000, over the last year.

Only 27,000 mortgages were released in November 2008, the lowest on record.

Perhaps now is the time for a sea-change in the way we think about our homes and ponder on how foolish we have been to treat them as win-win investments and personal piggy-banks.

Economic woes

The need for change is all the more compelling because the health of the world's economy is poor. Just as our bodies need to have a strong immune system to fight off diseases, so too must an economic system be robust enough to deal with unforeseens.

There are signs today that the world economic situation is far from being immune to, as yet unforeseeable, financial 'dis-ease'. In fact some economists fear that our resistance is terrifyingly low. With the world in the state it is, it will take only a relatively small insult to the body economic to lay us all low. Although there is no reason to believe that such a scenario will necessarily occur anytime soon, should China decide to stop investing in the west, for example, we would all catch a bad cold that could develop into pneumonia, such is our reliance on this single country's economic power.

At the time of going to press, there are signs that the downturn in UK property prices is accelerating into a full-blown recession. It could be claimed that with prices up threefold over the last decade it was about time for a correction. But however much one might wish this fall in prices would help hard-pressed first-timers, there's little evidence of them rushing in to pick up 'bargains' – if only because they can't borrow the cash to do so. And this is probably a good thing. Better they wait while the market settles, perhaps over the next year or two when they really *will* be able to get an affordable home.

Unfortunately, much media comment originates from economists and other gurus connected with mortgage banks and other lenders. It's obviously in their interests to talk up the market but their optimism (however guarded) over the last year or so seems ill-placed when looked at from where we are today. They also appear all too keen to talk the market *down* in an effort, perhaps, to prompt the Bank of England and other financial institutions to reduce borrowing rates and so maintain profit margins. Is it any surprise that most of us are confused about what is happening in what is already a very complex housing market?

These are just a couple of examples of the irresponsibility of these sources who, rather than being suitably cautious, chastened, or even pessimistic in an effort to redress the imbalances they have fostered over recent years, continue to 'fiddle while Rome burns'.

A part of this fiddling is the over-zealous reaction of most financial institutions to the very real shortage of money to lend. Their punitive lending criteria and higher charges are likely to cause even more grief for home-owners in the future than did their over-ambitious lending of the past few years. Bringing the home-buying market to a virtual standstill is no way to deal responsibly with the problem. Unless we take a root-and-branch look at the housing market, this current bust will produce yet another boom, followed by an even worse collapse in the future. Surely we can do better than this.

We are told that house prices fell by around 9% in the first half of 2008 – but it took 44 months for them to fall by 13% in the early 1990s when we last experienced such market turbulence. It's highly likely that by the time this book is in the shops, the UK housing market will be in free-fall. Yet anyone with a basic knowledge of economics could have foretold this, which is why some smart people deserted the housing market over the last two years.

The downturn we're living through is all the more tragic because what we've seen thus far is only the start of a much bigger story. The facts are that the UK housing market is so grossly over-valued that the depth of any necessary correction has been totally unpalatable to politicians and housing financiers alike. They fear talking the market into a recession but have done none of us any favours by being so timid. In fact, millions of householders, believing this hype, have held on, hoping – given the best information available to them – that they'd see things come good within a year or two. They are now set for a horrendous fall in the value of their homes. And that's if indeed anyone wants to, or can, buy them. After all, things only have a value when someone wants to buy them.

I would not be surprised if values were to fall by 50% over the period 2007 - 2011, taking inflation of between 1% and 3% into account. House prices have already fallen by 30% in Australia and by far more in many areas of the US. The return to pre-crash prices after the blood-letting of the early '90s in the UK took eight years. There's no reason to believe this downturn will recover any faster. In fact, there are good reasons to claim it could come back even more slowly, given the current global increases in food and fuel prices and the already apparent price rises and inflation that follow on from them.

Talking of inflation, some astute thinkers are concerned that no-one much mentions the subject. When the economy is going well and house prices are soaring, rising inflation doesn't too much matter. But it certainly matters, now. At first sight inflation might appear attractive in that it makes our debts smaller, especially when rates of interest are lower than inflation, but the downside is far worse. Inflation wrecks our savings; is hell for those living on fixed incomes (and they are getting more numerous year on year); forces wage demands upwards; and makes the provision of index-linked pensions in the public sector more costly, which affects us all as we have to foot the bill. Because of these undeniable factors, keeping inflation under control is a *must*, however bitter a pill it may be for politicians.

Even if house prices were not to fall too dramatically, and I'm sure they will, our homes will be worth less every year simply because of inflation. However much prices *actually* fall over the next few years, don't forget to take inflation into account when calculating the *real* value of your home.

During the month of November 2008 interest rates and inflation started to fall in the UK. In fact, some pundits were claiming we could be in for a period of deflation. Attractive as this may sound, it brings with it its own particular hazards, one of which is high levels of unemployment.

With unemployment rising, many people will be unable to afford the housing they want for some time. And this when about sixteen per cent of home-owners say they are depending on the cash locked up in their homes for their pension. With 18.5 million owner-occupied houses in Britain, this amounts to close-on three million homes. This could mean a rather different retirement from the one many had anticipated on releasing their much-reduced pension pot when selling their home.

The Ups and Downs of the Property Ladder will, I hope, give some insight into the realities of housing in the UK today and offer practical assistance to those who are trying to decide whether to buy, sell, rent or stay put in these turbulent times.

CHAPTER 1
BET YOU DIDN'T KNOW....
SOME FACTS AND
FIGURES OF UK
HOUSING

- There are around 25 million homes in the UK. Just over 70% of these are privately owned, about half with a mortgage and half outright; the rest are rented

- There are about 1 million empty properties of which about a quarter are empty homes

- The value of all the homes in Britain slumped from £6.1 trillion in September 2007 to £5.8 trillion in June 2008…..a loss of £1 billion a day

- The UK government has a set a target of 3 million more new homes by 2020. At the moment this goal looks very unlikely to be met

- In 2007, 167,577 new homes were built but this number is expected to fall in 2008 to 120,000 and to fall yet again in 2009 to the lowest level of housing construction since World War II

- At least 223,300 new households are expected to form each year between 2008 and 2026

- More than 1.5 million people are living in over-crowded homes and 1.7 million households (more than four million people) are on waiting lists for social housing

- The National Housing Federation has calculated that we are short of 70,000 new homes each year, for those in housing need alone

- Demand for housing is going up every year at a time when supply is going down

Huge demographic changes are also taking place in the UK.

- In 2008 pensioners outnumbered children for the first time. By 2031 there'll be fifteen million pensioners even though the pensionable age will have risen to 66, for both men and women, by 2024 and to 68 by 2050.

- Currently, 3.3 people of working age support every pensioner; this will fall to 2.9 by 2031, by which time the UK population is expected to have reached 71 million. Forty-seven per cent of this population increase will be comprised of immigrants but the positive side of this is that they will probably have more children than average and these children will, in turn, support the elderly of the future. In addition to this workforce, though, it will almost certainly, before too long, become necessary for us all to work until well into our seventies. After all, something will have to be done to increase the performance of the 'horse' while the 'cart' gets heavier!

These changes will have serious implications for all kinds of resources, but especially for housing.

Chapter 2
HOUSING AND HOMES...
AN EMOTIONAL ROLLERCOASTER

It is said that 'An Englishman's home is his castle'. This apparently simple statement masks underlying issues that make housing a compelling subject that goes well beyond the roof over our heads. After all, few would deny that a house and a home are different things. You rarely hear someone talking about losing their 'property', or their 'house'...it's always their 'home'. And when things go pear-shaped, lending institutions don't mind repossessing people's investments but very much do mind the emotional implications and PR backlash when they deprive a family of their 'home'.

The fascinating question is why we British have become so sensitive about our homes and why they hold such emotional significance for us. Could it be that somewhere in the collective unconscious we find succour in our real estate because of our shared social history?

Britain hasn't been invaded since 1066, which creates an entirely different mind-set compared with that in most other European countries – and not just about housing. Whereas the majority of European cities were fortified against invaders and people lived in close quarters behind safe city walls, the British never adopted this model on any large scale. In my view, it is this starting point that makes most Europeans happier to live in apartments close to one another whereas the British are more 'spaced-out' yet, paradoxically, more insular. This unconscious notion of 'shared space' has made most Europeans more relaxed about where they live and many Continental town and city dwellers see a lifetime of renting someone else's property as their home as entirely acceptable and desirable.

This is all thrown into fine focus when asking British people what they'd ideally like in a home. Almost all say, 'a three-bedroom, detached house with a small garden, front and rear'. Ask the immigrants arriving on our shores and their answer is, 'an apartment in the city where I can be near to everything'.

Perhaps the 'castle' which every Englishman claims he wants reflects the British craving for privacy and separation from others in line with the 'keep-yourself-to-yourself' attitude that so many people from other cultures remark on. In an ideal world, perhaps, and at some unconscious level, we crave a real drawbridge in our front gardens! In many ways we certainly create metaphorical ones. A 2008 study found that we scarcely talk to our neighbours any more. Even gossiping over the garden fence is virtually dead, with only one in five of those asked having any contact with their neighbours at all. Londoners were the least communicative and those living in Edinburgh the most friendly.

Housing in the UK is also governed by another factor, not much seen elsewhere and somewhat unacceptable to discuss – social class. Although class issues are declining in importance there's still an undercurrent that affects us all, however unconsciously. It's interesting that when many people make money they seek out traditional, even period, housing to display their wealth. By buying into this model they associate themselves with the (former) upper class. They are now the new 'squirearchy'. This tends not to be the case in most other countries, where the newly-rich have contemporary-style homes designed for them. There are British architects who design ultra-modern homes yet live in period houses themselves. As a nation we seem to yearn for the values of more 'emotionally comfortable', pre-industrial times. Ask any mass developer what sells and he'll tell you it's a style of architecture that resonates with our long-lost rural past!

The class issue also colours our views on renting rather buying a home. It is still seen as 'lower class' to rent....in contrast to Sweden, where it's possible and perfectly acceptable to move between the private rental, public rental and owner-occupied sectors, according to need or time of life. We are nowhere near this in the UK. Our housing tenure appears to define us in ways that are very basic and speak volumes about social class. I look at rental property in detail on page 80.

Needs and wants

Abraham Maslow, the American psychologist who died in 1970, made his name by creating what he called the Hierarchy of Needs. He asserted that we all need resources in life, from the most basic to the highly complex, if we are to survive and thrive. He created a graphic pyramid of these needs and took this as a guide for looking at how people function.

There are six layers to Maslow's pyramid.

On the base level are our needs for Shelter, Food, Water, Sex, and Sleep. In other words, matters that are largely to do with *Physiology*. We need these very things to stay alive and function physically.

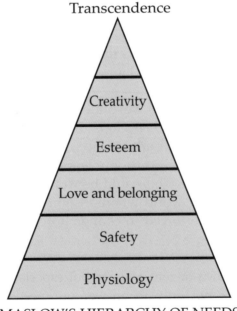

MASLOW'S HIERARCHY OF NEEDS

On the second layer are our needs for Security of body, Resources, Employment, Family and Property. This is his *Safety* level.

On the third layer are our needs for Friendship, Family and Intimacy. This is about *Love and Belonging*.

On the fourth layer are Self-esteem, Confidence, Achievement, and Respect from others. This is his *Esteem*.

On the fifth layer are Self-actualisation, Creativity, Morality, and Problem solving. What Maslow called *Creativity*.

Finally, there's the peak of the pyramid, our Spiritual needs. Maslow called these *Transcendence*.

It's clear from this list that as we ascend from the base of the pyramid we become less 'animal-like' and more intensely human.

But how is any of this of interest in a book about housing in these troubled times?

In my opinion, unless we understand the real issues behind our attitudes, conscious or unconscious, to our homes, we'll be at a disadvantage when dealing with the current crisis and will certainly learn nothing from it to take into the future. This could be worse than a nuisance in a fast-changing world where insight may be our only ally when we are forced to change how we think about our housing.

Whether we own or rent a home, but especially if we own one, we seek not only to answer our needs for shelter (Maslow's base level) but unconsciously also try to find a way of meeting many of our other needs. In a society in which large numbers of us are isolated from our families, and when the world seems increasingly alienating and hostile, our home becomes a place on to which we can, albeit unwittingly, project those of our needs that transcend those for shelter. We then set about answering them according to our unique and individual personality styles.

So, what started off simply as a place to live, soon becomes a place of Maslow's Safety; concerned with *Love and Belonging*; where we gain (or lose) *Esteem*; indulge our *Creativity*; and even experience levels of *Transcendence*.

This is a lot to ask of a dwelling.

It is only by being aware of the principles that underlie these needs that we can begin to understand why our homes are of such unusual significance to us as a nation.

The problem is that over the last few decades we have over-invested not only our wealth but also ourselves in our housing. As a result, when things start to go bad on the housing front, we over-interpret the 'loss' of the apparent solution to so many of our needs. The very fear and greed that drove and over-valued a bricks-and-mortar answer in the first place, are now being replaced by a fear and dread of their removal.

This makes turmoil in the housing market an uncomfortable place to be for many of us. Having unconsciously built too much emotional 'stuff' into our homes, and asked too much of them, we're now having to assess how we'll cope when threatened with their loss.

Although the picture is a highly complex one, I'll look at just a few of the main topics that came up time and again in the consulting room when I was dealing as a therapist with people in 'housing distress'. Of course, they never came in the door with this label, but whatever the ticket that brought them, it soon became apparent that it was at the heart of their problems.

Dealing with emotions

Money

Money is a strange commodity. It has value only because we say it does. What money does have, though, is many associated emotions lurking in the shadows that trouble most of us from time to time and can damage our intimate relationships. When divorced couples are asked what their main problem areas were when married, the majority reply, 'Money'.

Money means different things to different people. To some it signifies stability and security; for others, freedom to do what they want; some see it only as a problem if there's too little or too much of it; a few see it only as a way of being of service to others; some believe 'money is the root of all evil'; and yet others see it as a way of gaining and retaining power or respect.

The symbolism associated with money, or perhaps the symbolic power it confers on its owner, is far more significant than the money itself. Rich people really do get treated differently from the poor and money can indeed buy happiness even though those who have never been rich strive endlessly to convince themselves that it does not. Of course, not all rich people are happy but far more poor people are unhappy.

The trouble with money within intimate relationships, is that the two people involved often have different perceptions of what money is for. This leads to confusion and conflict when there's too little or too much of it around. It can also be a serious cause of friction if the status quo is threatened, as in a housing recession or an economic downturn. People's views on debt also vary hugely. There are those who feel terribly guilty or even ashamed if they have even a small overdraft. Some individuals are meticulous about paying bills while others think companies should wait for their money. Then there are savers and spenders. When things get tough and money is short, debt becomes a problem rather than a resource. This means that for millions of people today a shortage of money is becoming a daily concern – and for many this is an entirely new experience.

The truth is that the making, accumulating, taking care of and disposing of money causes friction in a substantial proportion of households. Add now a concern for the future and it's easy to see how the subject can become a mine-field in any relationship.

The trouble within most intimate relationships is that money is a bit like sex. Of itself 'sex' has no value, it is worth only what we say it is. But like money, it has the power to transform or impoverish relationships. It can be used well, abused, or used inappropriately. Sex can be bartered or traded for reasons that have nothing to do with sex itself. In other words, sex is like money in that its significance is largely symbolic .

In our culture it is often claimed that it's impossible to be 'too rich' or 'too sexy'. This belief brings penalties in both spheres of modern life.

When my partner spends more money than I'd like on the family, why do I feel so uncomfortable? How much money did anyone spend on *me* when I was a child? How did I feel about it? Would it be different if *I* were spending the money? What would we be spending it on if not on this? And so on.

Unfortunately, money is such a mine-field for many couples that they soon hit a 'no-go area' and retreat. The aggrieved individual sulks and acts out their anger and frustration, perhaps in the bedroom, and the issues go on hurting both parties for months or even years.

The only answer here is to calmly talk things through on the basis that our partner is our best friend who actually *isn't* trying to bankrupt, infantilise, or control us. Dealing with difference here can be very tough, though, because having enough money or being in debt isn't a matter of debate (as are care, love and affection). Unlike most other commodities we share in intimate relationships, money is embarrassingly finite!

Money matters seek out the realities of our relationships because, unlike the 'softer' commodities we daily trade between us, it is either there or it is not.

This small skirmish with the subject will, I hope, help get the ball rolling when thinking and talking about money at a time when it is proving a problem for millions of people who had not, until recently, found it to be one. That the current situation also involves our single most expensive and emotionally over-valued commodity – our home – only makes matters worse.

Change
One of the challenging topics that rears its head at times like this is change. Change is unavoidable. Change is a part of nature itself. We cannot pretend to ourselves that we can free ourselves from its tyranny, if this is how we see it.

Of all the things that change in our world, only one thing never changes.....our fear of change itself.

Most of us are happiest with the familiar. And this is no bad thing. After all, familiarity means not having to re-define the world every day. This saves time and energy. We have, after all, to be able to take many things for granted, or life would become intolerable.

In an ever-changing world, many of us think of our home as never-changing, at least unless it changes in ways we choose. How disappointing and frightening, then, to find that this rock is not what we imagined it to be. Change is now being thrust upon us by forces outside ourselves and it's not a good feeling. Infantile emotions of powerlessness, helplessness and hopelessness can now surface and, as in infancy when we couldn't control our world, we can get pretty distressed.

By definition, change means we have to start thinking and behaving differently. And this can be hard – unless we break down the necessary change into small, manageable units that we can deal with more easily. Making the whole change at once is far too big a mountain to climb but step by step the journey is possible. Unfortunately, as years as a therapist taught me, one person's small step can be another's Grand Canyon! Here again, we need to be gentle with one another in the family as we all feel and experience the threat of change differently. Some members will be exhilarated at the thought of moving home, perhaps even relieved that a decision has been forced on them. Others will fear any change at all, however good the outcome.

Most of us are afraid that change will, almost by definition, be for the worse. On balance, it isn't. In fact, it often improves our lives in ways we could never have foreseen. Having to move to a smaller house, or to a less expensive area, might seem a terrible blow but I'll be amazed if you don't eventually find some advantages. I know I have when similar changes have been thrust upon me.

After all, change is often simply an opportunity dressed up as a nuisance.

The goal now is to try to embrace change as a new beginning rather than the mortal threat it appears to be. It's also vital to do everything you can to make change happen at a pace you can dictate yourself. Far too many people, threatened with the loss of their home, go into 'headless chicken' mode or, even worse, into denial. Rather than grapple with the challenge of change, they cling on until things become so desperate that outsiders eventually take control, by which time they are powerless to influence the events that overwhelm their lives. When things look tough, there's no substitute for early action. Being pro-active will not just make you *feel* more powerful but will actually create positive results.

Loss

This is closely linked to change, as many of us fear that change will mean loss. Of course it *does* but whilst we'll undoubtedly lose *some* things we can also gain others. Bearing this in mind can inject just enough hope to make a seemingly bleak situation tolerable.

When we lose our home, or even if it's just the threat hanging over us, we tend to experience it as a death. It might seem strange to mourn the loss of our home before it's even gone – especially if it may never do so – but many of us do this unwittingly to prepare ourselves for what is to come. People say they do the same 'pre-mourning' when a relative or loved one is seriously ill. It can be the same when your home is 'seriously ill'.

There are several well-recognised stages in the grieving/mourning process:

- Denial – This can't be happening to me!
- Anger – Why is this happening to *me*?
- Bargaining – I promise I'll be a better person *if...*
- Depression – I don't *care* what happens any more
- Acceptance – I'm ready for whatever happens to me

Of course there's no actual script for grief or the threat of loss but these stages are experienced by most of us at one time or another.

In addition to these feelings, you may also be emotionally numb, become anxious, or get depressed. You'll know you're depressed if you:

- Feel sad
- Cry a lot
- Have little or no energy
- Don't enjoy the things you used to
- Go off sex
- Want to eat much more, or less
- Drink or smoke much more, or less
- Can't sleep
- Wake up very early each morning
- Have suicidal thoughts

If ever you have more than three of these symptoms, and especially if you feel suicidal, see your doctor. Most people threatened with the loss of their home, or when struggling to handle a financial crisis, feel low and some get actually depressed. Don't wait until things are really bad – get help sooner rather than later. This applies to those around you too, even if at first they seem reluctant.

When people are depressed, anxiety is never far away. And some of us are feeling almost permanently anxious as the credit crunch bites. People are worried about their investments; the effects of inflation on their future; and even about how safe their high street bank is. And this says nothing about the anxieties they have about their homes. The thing is that most people under about forty have never known a recession; have not been used to having people saying No to them; and have hardly experienced unemployment or redundancy. For this golden generation, 'hardship' is not a word with which they can easily connect. They have expected to 'have it all'. And, largely, they have.

But looking across the pond at our American cousins should be enough to make anyone in this group anxious. It's no longer only the poor 'sub-primers' who are losing their homes there: the middle classes are following fast. Evidence that a similar situation is on the way in the UK can be found in a helpline used by London's major banks and financial institutions which received 3,500 calls in the month of June 2008 alone from staff plagued by anxiety and depression.

As with depression, seek help sooner rather than later if you feel your level of anxiety is getting out of hand.

Stress
The credit crunch and all its manifestations are causing stress for millions. But what exactly is stress?

I find it helpful to draw a distinction between 'pressure' and 'stress'. Most of us say we function better under *some* pressure. Our expectations are higher, we try harder and we usually get better results. At some point, though, this pressure can escalate into something less positive. Both body and mind now start to suffer and we feel 'stressed'.

Of course, one person's pressure is often perceived by another as their idea of stress, and there are also many individuals in modern society who see stress as normal – which it should not be.

The problem is that with *real* stress we start to malfunction both physically and mentally. And concerns about money and the roof over our head are two very potent sources of this serious type of stress.

Some people actually thrive in stressful situations. It energises them and brings out all kinds of hidden skills and talents. They face crises well. Others cave in or become seriously unwell. Most of us fall somewhere between these two extremes.

For most of us in one-to-one relationships, the stress suffered by one can often be reduced by loving care, understanding, empathy and affection from our partner. However, when something hits us *both* at the same time, we may be unable to give the support the other needs as we're too busy fighting our own emotional fires. This is why failing domestic finances and housing problems are so damaging to relationships. Cracks now show in the relationship and self-blame, blaming our partner, guilt, shame, anger and fear, and all kinds of regressive behaviours can take us back to primitive emotional times in our lives. We now act child-to-child with our partner, or worse still, infant-to-infant and we can even start to question the very relationship itself. Cracks that had been papered over for years now open up.

People behave very differently under stress. Some take to drink or drugs; others get depressed; yet others gamble. Being continuously anxious or becoming physically ill are two other common responses. Sex usually suffers and this glue that held the relationship together becomes, at best, elastic. The sad paradox is that at times like this we all need more emotional and relationship glue, not less.

All of this can be far, far worse for those who started off with little in life. Many people don't function all that well under *normal* circumstances. Their social and coping skills aren't great at the best of times. For many millions, just coping day-to-day is hard enough, even before financial and housing problems hit them. Millions of ordinary, coping people function on the edge of their capabilities in life at the best of times. The credit crunch and its effects are now pushing such individuals to their limits. Some simply cannot cope.

But it's not just the 'poor souls' of society who are vulnerable. Many middle class and professional families have driven themselves to huge levels of self-imposed debt, living above their means. Their goals were set too high, their aspirations unrealistic.... unless buoyed up by huge debt based on the value of their over-valued homes. This section of the community will suffer increasingly, if only because they never imagined they'd find themselves in this position. Such households are also suffering from business downturns, reduced bonuses, and other financial woes from which they had thought themselves all-but immune. This can, in a way, be more stressful than the same events for those who had been disadvantaged from the start.

Modern life is bound to be stressful. And most of us will cope all right. Here are just a few tips that I've found over my years as a therapist to be effective. Try working on these alone, and also with a partner or a caring friend. If things are really tough, seek professional help.

- Eat healthily
- Reduce your caffeine intake
- Cut down on smoking and drinking
- Take daily exercise
- Get enough sleep
- Get at least half an hour of light out of doors each day
- Make time to play
- Spoil yourself
- Keep up your hobbies
- Spend time in meditation or prayer
- Boost your self-esteem
- Challenge your notions of 'shoulds' and 'oughts'
- Feel free to laugh, and cry
- Have realistic expectations
- Try to dwell on positives rather than negatives
- See the stressful situation as an opportunity to learn and grow
- Try to tolerate situations you can't change
- Separate thoughts from feelings
- Accept yourself
- Be assertive rather than passive
- Improve your decision-making skills
- Don't jump to conclusions or make assumptions
- Set realistic deadlines
- Nurture your one-to-one and other intimate relationships
- Keep your friendships going
- Ask for help, be it from family, friends and loved ones; or professionals, before things get desperate

Conflict and rows

In all human relationships, there's one thing of which we can be certain. There will be conflict. This is especially likely to be the case with our chosen life-partner because we unwittingly choose someone who is different from ourselves so we can work out our unconscious, 'unfinished business from the past' in our life with them.

When finances and housing start to become a worry, most of us find conflict is never far away. Even trying to decide exactly what's happening can cause conflict, working out how to respond creates more, and implementing changes that are forced upon us, yet more. It's hardly surprising that conflict raises its head if we look back at Maslow's needs (page 26). It is a rare couple whose needs and aspirations are met in exactly the same way by their home. They start out with different needs; meet them in different ways in their housing; and then respond differently when the going gets tough.

As with most things in life, prevention is better than cure. Clinical experience and research shows that couples who cope well with conflict in their lives:

- Continually encourage one another
- Have a bank of underlying goodwill on which they can draw
- Make time to enjoy what's good about their relationship
- Know how to resolve conflict early
- Have learned how to be open about practical, day-to-day issues

Successful couples detect early signs of conflict as if by a 'third eye' and then defuse it before it escalates into really serious trouble.

One way of doing this is to train ourselves to recognise our own emotions and to take responsibility for them, rather than projecting them on to our partner. Most of us create additional conflict, however unwittingly, by dumping our own anxiety, fear, frustration or rage, for example, on our partner. Hardly surprisingly, they don't want this and can get confused as to whether it's *their* stuff or *ours*.

These apparently simple preventives may sound a doddle but they're not. And even the most experienced couples find themselves in conflict from time to time. The more unconsciously attuned they are to the 'shadow' side of their partner, the fiercer this conflict will be. After all, a lot of the conflict we experience with others is just a reflection of that which rages within us. Because it's always harder to cope with these difficult issues within ourselves, we unwittingly project them on to our partner in the hopes that they'll somehow deal with them for us. This can, of course, occur. It's always possible to learn a lot from someone who deals with life's challenges differently. Usually, though, such projections are harmful and do nothing to get us out of trouble in difficult times.

One of the biggest problems I found when dealing with conflicted couples was their inability to distinguish fact from fiction. Most of us believe that because we think something is right, it *is* right! But this isn't true. The main difficulty with this approach is that the moment I believe I am right, by definition, you must be wrong if you disagree with me. If I am ego-centred, I'll then try to prove I am right and will insist on getting my own way, whatever the cost. If I am relationship-centred I don't much care whether or not I do this because my focus is the best outcome for us *as a couple*. In achieving this, I have, in reality, 'got my own way' – the way to a pleasant, harmonious and growing life.

The truth is that when we experience conflict we are usually *both* right....though from our own perspective. None of us has a direct line to the 'Truth' but when the going gets tough between us we tend to believe we do. This apparently self-protective response in fact harms our relationship. And when our backs are against the wall, our partner may very well be our best ally, whatever appears to be the case. We simply cannot afford to kill them off emotionally or we'll have to face life's dramas or crises alone.

Here are a few of the things you can do to prevent conflict.

- Try to separate out whose stuff is whose
- Remember you are *both* probably right
- Keep on finding reasons to encourage and praise one another
- Listen at least as much as you talk
- Work out between you how to manage compromise
- Detect conflict early and defuse it
- Negotiate, so you end up with a win-win situation whenever you can
- Never use threats to get your own way
- Never make assumptions about your partner based on yourself
- Try not to 'punish' your partner
- Prevent arguments and disagreements from growing into rows
- Never forget your partner is your best friend

In this section I've only skirted around the main emotional challenges that the current housing crisis can bring. If at any time you feel you're not coping, or that your relationship is suffering, get help sooner rather than later.

CHAPTER 3
HOW TYPICAL IS THE UK OF THE REST OF EUROPE?

We have seen how the British think about their homes and how this colours the property market. But how different are we from the rest of Europe?

North versus south

The problem with any such discussion is that 'Europe' isn't a distinct entity...it's a collection of individual countries, each with its own culture and practices, especially when it comes to housing. Southern European countries have, by and large, the highest home-ownership figures. Spain, Greece and Italy, for example, have levels of more than 80% while in Germany only 40% own their own homes. Ireland is an anomaly, as it has a 78% owner-occupier rate, yet it is a northern country. I look at this more below. It is often claimed that Britain's level of ownership is exceptionally high, but this is not the case, though with 70% of people owning their homes, it certainly comes in the top group.

A problem with all such statistics is that in some countries the data include all privately-owned homes, whether or not they are occupied. But this masks second home ownership, for example. This said, the proportions remain largely accurate when looked at on a large scale.

No one knows for sure why so many Germans rent their homes but one suggestion is that after World War II there was such a shortage of housing in Germany that people were forced to lived in rented homes, many of which were supplied by large industrial concerns for their workers. Also, without doubt, in high-renting countries such as Germany there is, and has never been, any stigma attached to renting. In the UK, 'council housing' has always been seen as a down-market option and something from which to escape if at all possible and even the private rental sector has been unpopular for several decades. This appears to be a largely British phenomenon when looked at over Europe as a whole although, of course, many people in 'social' housing in various countries would rather own, given the opportunity. Over recent years, France, for example, previously a very rental-friendly culture, has started to follow the British model of home-ownership. The changing pattern and availability of private rental housing in the UK is slowly altering perceptions on renting as a life-time option but it's very unlikely that attitudes to renting (as opposed to buying) in the UK will change dramatically within two generations. I look at everything to do with rented housing in more detail on page 80.

Some of the cultural differences within Europe are based on local custom and practice. In many southern European countries, families buy a home for their young people and, until as recently as the 1980s, a Greek girl would have been given a dowry home on marriage. The picture also differs and is influenced by things such as supply and demand, tax issues, and planning and construction constraints.

Obviously those countries with a sophisticated lending system also fare differently from those in which families are a main source of cash for first-time buyers' homes.

Until the 1980s, southern countries didn't have a very well-developed lending sector but this could have been influenced by the fact that it took so long to sell a home there, thus making it unattractive to lenders as they found it hard to get their money back on default. In fairness, there also wasn't the demand when families sorted things out between themselves. In northern countries, where families are no less caring, the lending system is so well developed that, combined with high house prices, families are neither needed, nor can afford to be as helpful as in the south.

Countries also differ in how long their young people stay in full-time education, and thus the average age at which they enter the property market. This is to a large extent governed by political objectives. Young people in southern countries tend to live at home for many years longer than do northern Europeans, which puts them in a better position, savings and earnings-wise when they eventually buy their first home. I see this in the Republic of Ireland where I live a lot of the time. Many people in their thirties are still living at home, especially in rural areas, and can build up considerable financial resources for when they eventually buy. The same kind of picture can also be found in Spain.

It might, at first, seem logical to expect that rich countries would have higher-than-average home ownership rates but the reverse is the case. Perhaps houses are just too expensive in rich countries. Property prices have risen dramatically in the Republic of Ireland and Spain over recent years and many people are currently saddled with huge mortgage debt. This used not to be the case up to twenty years ago.

Prior to this, both countries were relatively poor. In poorer European countries today, where home ownership is highest, the level of mortgage debt is lowest. The Republic of Ireland straddles the statistics in being a rich, northern country with huge mortgage debt, high levels of ownership and where higher-than-the-average numbers of young people live at home for a long time. Scandinavia has the lowest proportion of adult youngsters living at home. In Italy and Spain, even with no dowry system, many families are still involved in financing the housing of their young.

What? No property ladder?

Housing mobility is also very different in various European countries. By and large, people in southern countries move less frequently. There is generally no concept of a property ladder on to which you have to get a foothold and then struggle to climb. Young people tend to buy a home that will last them for many years, perhaps for the whole of their family life. This has to do with their 'property' being seen as a home rather than the 'investment' we've become used to in northern countries.

Once the concept of a 'ladder' exists it becomes vital to get on to it so as not to be left behind. This is also financially compelling when prices are rising, because there appears to be no better way of gearing debt to make a gain. If you're borrowing at five per cent and your home is going up by twice that percentage-wise, it's better than working for a living! The property ladder concept has meant that young British people buy as soon as they can possibly afford to, stay put for as short a time as possible then, as they earn more, and can thus borrow more, they move up the ladder to the next rung. But with the huge rises in prices we've seen over the last twenty or so years, it's now very common for young people to be in at least their early thirties before they can set their foot on the first rung. And with increasingly expensive money and less of it around to borrow the rental market will remain the only option for those who cannot live with their parents. This is set to change further as the credit crunch bites.

A well-recognised facet of the property ladder, in a rising market, is that people are tempted to buy homes that are too large for them. 'The bigger the home, the bigger the investment and thus the bigger the potential gain', has been the argument. But this artificially boosts the cost of living space and is already looking like folly as some such over-sized-home owners now search for smaller places. Paradoxically, it could be that as such down-sizers compete with those who can afford only a modest home, demand for, and thus the prices of, these smaller homes could soar – further debilitating first-timers and young families.

Because of the pressures of the property ladder, the UK and The Republic of Ireland now have the highest turnover rates of property anywhere in Europe – or at least they did before the current downturn. Given the way southern Europeans see their homes, such a property ladder is unlikely to take hold on a mass scale, except in larger towns and cities where other social and economic factors come into play. This said, as the downturn bites, the Council of Mortgage Lenders in the UK has suggested that 2008 would see the lowest level of property transactions for at least thirty years. Clearly, things are changing fast.

The property ladder is also exceptionally strong in the UK because people like to demonstrate their wealth in the form of housing. Perhaps this is a throw-back to the eighteenth and nineteenth centuries, with the growth of the country estates of newly-rich industrialists. Ever since the industrial revolution of these times, the affluent middle classes have flaunted their wealth by constructing large, showy homes. I've lived in both Germany and France at various times – in both countries with wealthy families. Not only did they happily rent, they had no concept of moving simply because their business or professional life was going well. They may have bought a second home but even then they tended to spend surplus earnings on things other than bricks and mortar. I was surprised when working in Sweden some years ago to discover that about half the population had access to a second home….though only half owns a first one!

While thinking about second homes, in the UK it is possible that they could contribute to the crash in house prices. It appears that as many as a quarter of second-home owners could be forced to sell in the current downturn, prompting even more serious house price falls. Around a quarter of a million English households have second homes that are not rented out as buy-to-lets. The number of second homes fell by a quarter during the last recession, in the early '90s. The current sell-off will be further affected by changes in capital gains tax introduced by the UK government in April 2008, which reduced this tax from 24% for a higher rate tax payer to 18%. This is an incentive to sell for those who find themselves in financial trouble with their other investments. However, there may not be enough cash in the banks and interest rates may be too high to tempt buyers to pick up these gems. The result will probably be a fall in prices, which will necessarily knock on to the day-to-day property market. After all, one person's second home could quickly become a local person's main one – if it's at the right price. Unless you absolutely have to sell your second home, it's probably best to stay put. If, as is the case for many, you put down a fair chunk of cash in the first place, your exposure shouldn't be too great. And the loss is only a paper one until you sell, so it's best to ride out the storm if you can.

Just under half a million Britons have a second home overseas. Some of these are under siege from rising fuel prices. Low-cost airlines are cutting flights, making these homes harder to get to and thus less attractive as investments or re-sales. Having a low-cost airline near a second home can raise its value by 37%, according to Savills. Falling values of such assets will put large numbers of middle-class families under pressure, irrespective of what's happening with their home in the UK.

But home ownership to the average Brit is more than just a way of flaunting wealth and achievement. Over a generation the British have taken the idea of a family nest and expanded it to become a pension fund; a sort of private bank; a way of expressing their increasingly confident personalities; a hobby; a life adventure, and much more.

Supply and demand

Supply varies a lot from country to country and from time to time. In the 1980s Margaret Thatcher encouraged home ownership in the UK and made it possible for people living in council homes to buy at a considerable discount and subsequently sell off the housing they had occupied. This started a whole new trend in borrowing and the way it was perceived. It is probably fair to say that up until then most people would rather not be seen to be in debt....in fact there was something of a stigma attached to it. With Thatcher's aim of everyone becoming a home owner as a basic right, the accumulation of debt became not only possible but also highly desirable. Tax allowances followed that gave those borrowing for their homes advantages over those who did not. It thus became more sensible to buy than to rent…..especially as the selling off of one and a quarter million homes from the social rented housing stock meant that there was now very little left to rent! As a result, home ownership levels soared to its present seventy per cent and to be in debt became fashionable.

Some newcomers to the EU have recently privatised some of their housing stock, with the result that in Hungary, for example, ninety per cent of all houses are owner-occupied.

In Germany since World War II the government has gone the other way entirely, encouraging renting and discouraging buying. Nearly sixty percent of people rent from public or private landlords. Obviously, the supply of rental property affects the demand for homes to buy and vice versa. If it's difficult or expensive to buy (as it is in Germany and the UK today during the current credit crunch) then renting looks more attractive. In The Republic of Ireland, owner occupation has fallen from about 80% to 77% over only a few recent years, for this same reason.

But just because Germany has such a high rental rate doesn't mean that Germans don't like home ownership. They do. But because of highly restrictive planning laws, land is difficult to come by and thus expensive. The Germans are also known for their high standard of building which, in turn, keeps house prices very high. This has given rise to situations in which someone might own a home yet choose to rent it out and rent another one in which to live. Tax advantages make this sensible.

An almost polarity-opposite of this can be seen in Belgium. Belgians have, until recently, been encouraged to buy small plots of land and develop them for single-family homes. This has been going on for generations. The situation was entirely a result of planning laws that made it desirable and easy for people to build what they wanted. Of course this also kept mass developers out of the game.

Talking of supply and demand, France has a 9% surplus of housing stock at a time when the UK has a 9% deficit.

Planning restrictions also affect the price and availability of houses. By rationing the amount of land that can be built on, not only land values but also the price of the houses built on it, are artificially raised. Obviously, central and local governments in every country have a huge say on planning and thus, indirectly, on the cost of their housing stock. This means that house prices are directly related to such political thinking.

There's little doubt that as the European adventure progresses and centralised European bodies control more and more of everyone's daily lives as a result of legislation such as the proposed Lisbon Treaty, the property differences between countries will slowly even out. As more relatively rich people move freely between the various jurisdictions when buying second homes and investing in businesses, they'll spread their wealth and raise local people's expectations. Perhaps over the next decade or two, property behaviour and attitudes that are currently seen mainly in the UK and certain other northern European countries will spread to affect all twenty- seven. And perhaps these very same countries will look carefully at what they can learn from those cultures that rent their homes. We all have something to learn from our neighbours.

Chapter 4
HOW THE DOMESTIC PROPERTY MARKET WORKS

There are several ways in which people are housed in the UK. About one third of households own their homes outright; just over a third own them with a mortgage; and the others live in private or public rented accommodation. Let's look first at owner-occupiers.

Owner-occupied housing

Over the years since World War II it has become fashionable to own your own home if you can.

Before World War I only about ten per cent of people in the UK owned their homes (with or without a mortgage). The figure reached 49% in 1971 and now stands at 70%. It is unlikely that this will increase much in the near future.

For many decades over the last half century, those who chose and could afford to buy a home did so and lived in it for many years. Historically, house prices tended to keep pace with inflation and things were fairly comfortable for those who owned.

Over the last thirty-or-so years, though, the situation has changed dramatically as property prices have broken free from their relationship with inflation. At a time when inflation was in very low single digits, some properties inflated by up to one hundred per cent per annum. At the same time people's incomes didn't rise at this speed so the house-price-to-income ratio changed as never before.

Over the past fifteen years since the recovery from the previous property recession (in the early 1990s), people's homes, or their 'properties' as they, significantly, started to call them, became the subject of endless dinner-party banter, and suddenly everyone was a property expert. Most home-owners were 'earning' more from their home's inflation than they were from working. This gain was only a paper one, of course, but that didn't seem to matter. The media picked up on this with its numerous property-based TV shows. And rather as with sex, where everyone who has ever had a relationship feels competent to hold forth on the matter in general, we bred a nation of people who'd never seen a property downturn, let alone a crash, yet thought of themselves as property gurus!

It was, until about 2006, generally held that money, be it your savings or your pension fund, was safer in bricks and mortar than anywhere else.

Those of us who had seen two previous major property crashes before, weren't so sure. In central London, in an area where I later lived, property lost one third of its value and took eight years to come back to its pre-crash prices. So much for the safety of bricks and mortar! Those who had had no experience of such events, and even, I have to say, some who had, firmly believed that the housing market could go only one way. Up.

They were in for a shock.

This attitude is, however, understandable. Many people with no previous experience of dealing in property – and certainly no concept of what being a true property investor entails – rode the tidal wave and declared themselves 'investors', flipping properties, acquiring buy-to-lets and making substantial profits. In reality they were simply opportunists who happened to be experiencing a unique bubble in the housing market....and happily rode it.

As the saying goes, 'All boats float on a rising tide'.

Along with this came a kind of mass delusion and arrogance that seemed to assert that everyone was on a roll and that no-one could lose. If you didn't play the game you were a mug, and would get left behind. This easily-made (paper) money fuelled the delusion that millions of us had, even though the fundamentals underlying the whole game were seriously flawed. Estate agents poured fuel on to this fire and eventually a furnace evolved that generated so much heat no one could see the light! Greedy lenders connived with greedy borrowers and we built a very shaky structure indeed.

All this has to be set against the more general picture of what we could have done with our money at the time. Low interest rates meant poor returns from ordinary savings and the stock market wasn't thrilling, despite its greater flexibility, so people looked to the property market for results. But the truth is that one sector of the economy simply cannot be relied on to continue producing the goods in this way. For example, as soon as interest rates rise, or other asset classes become attractive, people will save again in other ways.

Easy money

Over the last decade or so money has been cheap to borrow – and plentiful. And in a society with very low unemployment this meant that ordinary, median-income families could afford bigger loans than had been previously possible. Falling interest rates offset rising house prices and allowed ever-costlier houses to remain within the reach of ordinary families. So even though most people had a larger mortgage, and more of other types of debt leveraged against their homes, their monthly repayments didn't give them much pain because low interest rates and the rising equity in their bricks and mortar provided a sense of comfort. If the worst came to the worst, they argued, they had substantial equity in their homes and would be OK.

What has happened since the late summer of 2007 is that this flow of easy money has dried up. And the financial institutions are to blame. After the last recession, those of us involved in property were wringing our hands: as the very institutions which had over-lent in the previous decade and swore they never would again, were now showering people with cheap loans. It was obvious that we were being set up for another fall.

Over recent decades, it was usual for lenders to give about three times a borrower's income as a home loan. I look at this in more detail on page 217. Over the last decade or so this changed as lenders sought new markets from which to make money. They started to lend to sectors of the community that really couldn't afford a home loan unless things were 'massaged' somehow to 'prove' that they could. This was the birth of the so-called 'sub-prime' (poor-quality) mortgage market. It started in the US and soon came to the UK. Institutions also started 'forcing', or rather 'enticing', existing borrowers to take on larger debts.

On both sides of the Atlantic millions of would-be home-owners and re-mortgagers were seduced into taking out huge loans, sometimes up to ten times a joint annual salary.

It's important to bear in mind when thinking about all this that lenders don't supply mortgages to borrowers from the income they receive from savers. They do, of course, do this but they also sell on their mortgage debts to other financial institutions, so as to share the risk. And they borrow from others too. I don't think most, even quite financially aware, people realised this until the recent 'credit crunch'. This colourful term relates to the implosion of financial institutions who found themselves in a terrible position. The poor-quality loans they'd made to unsuitable customers were starting to go bad on them and they lost fortunes as these borrowers couldn't repay them. Cynics amongst us had claimed earlier that such outfits lent money to poor-quality borrowers in the knowledge that if they couldn't keep up with their payments they, the institutions, would still have the property and could sell it on for more money in a rising market. In other words, it looked as if they couldn't lose. Of course this hasn't happened, because prices have fallen. They are reaping their own harvest on this and some unscrupulous outfits in the US will see their directors sent to jail. Alas, many others have made fortunes at arm's length from these easily-named individuals and are sitting on huge piles of ill-gotten cash while millions of families suffer.

But in the short term, US lenders are repossessing properties and having to sell them at massive losses. I personally know of developers and entrepreneurs who are picking up bargains in the US from such sources. It is possible, at the time of writing, to go on bus tours round repossessed US properties, cherry picking from what's available.

In the light of all this, the easy money suddenly dried up as the financial institutions found they had lost far more than they'd dreamed possible. Their greed and drive for lending growth had come back to bite them. Unfortunately, and tragically, it has hurt us all.

But this isn't all. Because of the legal situation in the US which means that if you cannot pay your mortgage the lender can take your house back from you yet not claim anything else, some people, even though they can afford to pay their mortgage, seeing their increased monthly payments funding a diminishing asset, are simply walking away from their homes, leaving their lenders with the reduced-value house to sell. This is creating a massive level of loss in the financial institutions which, it has been estimated, could eventually amount to more than one trillion dollars. Of course people will still need to be housed, so it could be that these cheap homes will be re-circulated in other ways. But whatever happens to the properties themselves, the losses for the major lenders will be astronomic. This will affect us all, on both sides of the Atlantic, in ways that are, as yet, hard to predict.

Employment

Few things influence house prices more than employment, or rather a lack of it. However low interest rates are, you can't borrow if you are unemployed. In Japan, for example, where interest rates are minute, the property market has been stuck in a rut for more than a decade because the economy (and thus employment) is stagnant.

At its most obvious level, local markets can suffer terribly when a major employer leaves the town or shuts down. What happens in a property bubble, though, is that once the over-heated economy – based on the value of what people perceive they have as 'fat' in their homes – starts to erode, consumer confidence wanes, we all stop spending, businesses fail and people lose their jobs. Although this behaviour is rooted to some extent in reality, consumer sentiment plays a vastly bigger part. As we all feel poorer, with rising fuel prices, borrowing costs and food bills, and things seem bleak for the future, it feels sensible to hold on to our money. Paradoxically and, perhaps, predictably, given the theme of this book, the housing market is looking exempt from this. There are signs, at the time of going to press, that those who can find the cash are putting it into improving their homes in the belief that it'll be an investment that will reap rewards again one day. I hope they are right.

But they may not be. It could be that after the dust has settled from this recession, given the state of the world with global warming fears, oil price rises, and even food shortage scares, house prices may never rise again in the way they did. We could, in my view, be in for a Japanese-style housing market which is virtually stagnant pricewise, even if the economy performs well and most of us have jobs. In this sense I think we're in a totally different place from the mid-1990s when we bounced back from the property crash, albeit over several years. Social attitudes have also changed, especially among the young.

A counter argument to this assertion is that in a society where there is such a shortage of homes, this alone will keep prices high. Over the next five years we shall see which turns out to be the case.

I know that the proposition that housing may never again be the cash cow we have recently experienced will seem sacrilegious to those who have become used to their home's increased value making them feel rich, but it won't to the millions who rent for a lifetime, for whom their home isn't an 'investment'. I look at rented housing in much more detail on page 80.

That unemployment is becoming a serious issue at this time is no longer a matter of debate. The number of UK companies served with county court judgements or winding-up petitions rose six-fold in the first four months of 2008, and with banks lending ever-less to businesses, this figure is rising. The same study found that in south-east England 2,301 companies were tagged as 'critical' in the first four months of 2008 compared with 387 during the same period in 2007. Any business exposed to discretionary spending knows it is looking at a downturn and thus a loss of jobs. At the moment many high-end businesses are feeling good, and haven't yet experienced much of a fall-off in trade but this could change in a heartbeat. There are signs that even the super-rich are feeling the pinch.

As unemployment rises, more people will be unable to afford to service their debt and house prices will fall for this reason, whatever happens to mortgage availability or interest rates. Interest rates are in fact rising, making monthly repayments more unaffordable for ordinary families who, at the same time, stand a greater chance of losing their jobs. It's not that companies are any less efficient or creative than they were, it's simply that without customers they cannot survive, however good their products or services.

This is why the current housing crisis is, in the opinion of many experts, far more serious than previous crashes since World War II. The level of personal indebtedness is the highest on record and most of us are working too close to the financial bone for comfort. Add to this the certainty of everything rising in price as China and India, for example, make increasing demands on global resources and we're in for a totally different scenario from the 1990s.

The only way things will resolve, in my view, is for house prices to fall dramatically, perhaps by up to 50% in real terms (allowing for inflation of, say, 1-3% a year) over the years 2007-2011. This will make housing less expensive for those trying to get started in their first home but will cause untold grief and even tragedy for millions of others. Quite how the financial institutions will cope with such vast levels of un-repayable debt remains to be seen. The US government has already had to step in to support the two largest US suppliers of mortgage money to lenders and without a doubt more such rescue missions will be needed. In the UK, the government came to the rescue of Northern Rock, a bank that over-stretched itself in the mortgage business. Every time we hear bad news from the financial sector we ask ourselves how many more Northern Rocks there will be on which the government could founder. As I go to press, household-name high-street banks are being bailed out by governments and tax payers around the world, with unpredictable consequences in both the long and the short term.

Why a house costs what it does

Housing is rather different from most other commodities we're used to buying in modern society. And it is this difference that affects its price. We've become accustomed to consumer goods getting better and costing less every year. The minute we buy a car, its value falls. Try selling a second-hand TV, or furniture. The manufacturers can easily make more, though, so there's no problem. UK housing doesn't behave like this.

Supply and demand. At a simplistic level, it would seem sensible to suggest that when housing is in short supply its price will rise. And at a very local level this is true. It might make sense to point out here that there is no such thing as 'the housing market'. In effect, the 'market' is a mass of small sub-markets. There are two general things, though, about supply. First, there's the existing stock of housing. This affects house prices because aged and redundant housing is constantly being removed from the market, thus increasing the value of the remaining stock, if sufficient replacements aren't built. In addition to the one million empty dwellings in the UK, hundreds of thousands more are taken out of the market every year as they come to the end of their lives. This proportion will rise exponentially as time goes by because although a Victorian-built house might last another 100 years, the average home built today will have a life of only about 60 years! At first this might appear to be a disadvantage but it may not be, provided there's enough new house building. A developer I know has recently commissioned the construction of an old people's home to have a life of only 25 years. This is because the likelihood of regulatory changes over that period rendering it unusable is so high that it pays to take a short-term view. After all, the land will still be there and able to be 're-cycled' for a more appropriate building. This type of thinking could also apply to housing in general as requirements for sustainability and greenness overtake us.

Existing homes are also taken out of circulation for redevelopment of many kinds, including retail parks, roads, schools and so on.

Building and land costs. New construction is the only true source of supply of new homes. But, unlike with a computer gaming console, the market can't respond quickly to the demand for new homes: planning for and building them takes years, by which time the demand could be different, or the demand could be for different things, or the same things in different places.

House construction costs also increase year by year, sometimes by much more than inflation.

It is often claimed that Britain is short of homes because it is a small country that has too little land to develop. This is complete nonsense. Although the 'green belt' is treated as if it were sacrosanct, it should not be. Few people realise that 90% of all the land in England is undeveloped. Even if we were to expand all our urban areas by ten per cent we would still only develop one more per cent of the countryside.....leaving 89% still undeveloped. If we are failing to build enough new homes, it is not because of a land shortage. It's because of other issues I'll look at soon – all of which inflate the cost of land, and thus of housing.

If we consider mass market housing, the costs are easy to compute. Let's say a developer has a piece of land and wants to make money by building on it. Valuers tell him exactly what he can charge per unit in the current marketplace. He then talks to the planners and does deals in order to get the largest number of these units he can on his site. This might involve some horse-trading ('I'll give you a bit of my land for your roundabout if you let me have more houses') but whatever happens the developer can now set the price for the houses. He knows what he paid for the land and knows he wants to make about thirty per cent profit in return for his risk and effort. The selling price falls out of this simple equation. He knows what it costs per square metre to build such housing and he can thus project his profits even before a brick is laid.

But all this depends on two things: first, that he can buy land at a price that reflects and, paradoxically, drives the final value of the houses he builds and second, that he can, in fact, sell what he builds. Very few builders use their own money to create a housing estate. They borrow, like the rest of us! This means that their fixed costs are huge and that they have to sell a substantial proportion of the estate, or flats in a block, before they recoup their costs (or can even borrow more money to complete the project), let alone see a penny profit. They also hold large land banks, some of which are being paid for with borrowed cash, and have high fixed overheads in the shape of their workforce, capital equipment, offices, loans to be serviced, and so on.

All of this makes mass market housing a fairly tricky business. When things are going well it's possible to make a lot of money but when they are not, it's easy to lose even more.

And, of course, houses built five years from now will cost more to construct, while second-hand housing, because of its shortage, will rise in value proportionately. In any sensible market, second-hand housing by definition costs less than new – as with a car. But this only pertains to markets where new things can be manufactured very quickly and easily, which is not generally true of housing in the UK. The way around the UK's housing shortage, which looks set to get much worse over the next thirty years, is to build more. But even before the credit crunch, developers, land-owners and the government were loath to do this because to do so would reduce the value of everyone's existing home. The price of land is kept unrealistically high by the reluctance of land owners and land bank holders to release it too readily (as the longer they hold on to it the more valuable it becomes); the green movement that doesn't want to see greenfield sites developed; and the planners who have their own objectives and reasons for not allowing as much building as we need. These, and other influences, maintain high land prices that then drive the eventual price of the homes built on it. If, to be whimsical for a moment, the government were to nationalise all land and the price were to fall dramatically, new homes would cost a fraction of what they currently do, but everyone's existing home would fall in price too, with serious and unacceptable side-effects for the electorate.

Availability of finance. At the moment, major house builders can't sell their stock because most people can't get mortgages. They themselves are also finding money hard to obtain. As a result, most developers have severely cut back their output and many have even shut sites entirely. Few are buying more land. They are doing everything they can to induce buyers to part with their cash, but without any great success. They can discount to a certain degree but not enough to get themselves out of trouble. Most are trying to cut costs, re-finance, and keep their heads down while they await a recovery. Some will not survive the wait. Insiders I know claim that it'll all end in tears as Indian, Chinese, Russian and Middle-Eastern companies come in for the kill and hoover up the UK's ailing house-building giants.

At a time like this, it's clear that anyone selling their home will be up against these big players who are desperate to sell their stock. This is why, if you have to sell in this market, you'll have to be a whole lot better at it than you would have been two years ago. I look at this in detail on page 107.

Another thing that affects supply and demand is liquidity....how much money is out there looking for a home in the housing market. When property is going well everyone wants a piece of the action. When, like now, it is not, then smart money gets out. In all market-driven situations there are people known as 'early adopters'. These people get in on trends quickly, take risks, then get out early. This applies to those who buy the first plasma TVs, or build an eco-home. Early adopters in the current property market took their cash out of housing in 2006 and are now renting while their cash earns interest in a bank. They'll stay put until the market has bottomed out (but who knows how to judge this?) and then buy back in again. In general, such people read property bubbles well and know that the fastest-growing ones pop soonest. Whether as investors or as home-owners, such people get out fast and early.

Levels of employment. On the demand side for housing, jobs are the greatest single driver. Jobs drive the property market at both domestic and commercial levels. Unfortunately, the jobs equation isn't an equal one. Jobs go quickly but come back very slowly. This greatly affects the property market.

Interest rates. As most of us borrow to buy our homes, interest rates are important when it comes to affordability. Lowering interest rates has the same effect as increasing our income. Low interest rates also drive up prices. Most people say they want to see interest rates fall but there's a compelling case for the opposite. Proponents of this approach claim that although higher rates would mean more repossessions, and more bankruptcies, at this time in the housing cycle we need to calm things down because there's no such thing as true economic growth if it is based on people and businesses living beyond their means. Painful though it will be, allowing the property market to slow down and find a healthier, stable level is definitely the way to go. Almost anything the government could do to interfere in this process could have more negative effects than positive ones.

At the most simplistic level, governments bailing out (or even nationalising) banks may help in the short term but we, the tax payers, are now being saddled with debts that have never before been seen in peace time. However compelling it may be to salvage the current financial crisis this way and even to prevent a true economic depression, we are undoubtably storing up problems for the future. Eventually, the way things are going, people will start to wonder whether even governments are a safe place to keep their money (in bonds) and then we'll start to see whole countries going bankrupt.

The need for more homes. The growth in numbers of households (rather than population growth *per se*) also drives demand and affects prices in a market where the pace of new building doesn't keep up. As more of us nowadays are single; divorced; widowed or separated; and tend, on average, to be living longer, there's a growing demand for more, smaller homes.

Over many years there's been a relatively steady and rather slow relationship between the supply and demand for housing. Interest rates, jobs and what people earned roughly balanced each other....acknowledging, as I do, the fact that we need more homes overall in the UK. But whatever this global shortage, when money gets tight and demand for homes falls, you can't suddenly get rid of thousands of homes and pretend they don't exist. So what's left becomes worth less. A good indicator of this happening is the time it takes to sell your home. In troubled times this lengthens. Houses still sell, of course, but for less money and they take much longer to do so.

Is it a good time to sell?

Unless you have to, I'd say no. Don't forget that whatever loss you think you may have made, it is never a real one until the day you sell. I suggest you put this day off for as long as you can. For some people this isn't possible, of course, as they need to trade down to release capital to pay off debts; or to create opportunities for other purchases (such as to buy a holiday or retirement home, or to help their children with their first home). If at all possible, though, find ways of staying put (see page 147).

It can be tempting to sell before the market slumps even more, then to rent and then buy back in later. But for most of us this isn't as easy as it sounds. It takes a long time to sell a house in a poor market; it's inconvenient when it's your home; and it costs a lot in energy, nerves, professional fees and taxes. The chances are you'll also be going down-market in your interim home. Is this really what you want? It's important, too, to remember that if you have a mortgage and sell up, you might not be able to get one for your new place when you want it. Some lenders will let you put your mortgage on hold for a fixed time but even this could change as lending gets tighter. In this context, the best mortgage is the one you already have. Spend your time and energy making more money to pay for it so you can ride out the downturn.

If you want to sell, you'll already have lost (on paper) some of your value, given that the downturn has been going for some time now. Add to this the costs of selling, renting, moving, storage and buying again, and this could all come to more than you think. Sit down and cost everything out before deciding to sell. I look at all the costs involved in selling, on page 138 and in buying on page 207. But all this assumes you're great at reading the market. Deciding when to get out and when to jump back in can tax even seasoned property professionals. You could find it near-impossible.

Unless you really have to go this route, or you're using it as part of a life-changing plan such as retirement; down-sizing; moving to a cheaper area etc that you would have done anyway, it's best avoided.

If you do decide to sell, it could be a fairly good time if you're trading up because the new home you'll want will have fallen by a lot more than yours in absolute terms. It's always best, in these circumstances, to concentrate on the difference between what you can sell for and what your new place will cost, rather than fixing your gaze on the headline price you may have in your head from before the crash. You'll still need to find the funds to buy, though which could be hard. If you're thinking of trading down, you'll be taking a loss, which could seriously affect any lump sum you intended to use as a pension, or for any similar purpose.

When setting your price, bear in mind that buyers will still want to do a deal, so be prepared for this by pricing in a way that allows you to reduce with dignity. However, even cutting your price dramatically may not work if there are things going against your property.

Helpful websites include:
    www.housepricecrash.co.uk
    www.propertysnake.co.uk
    www.globalhousepricecrash.com

Is it a good time to buy?

Not unless you're down-sizing to clear your debts, need to release capital for some other purpose, or were intending to move to a much cheaper area anyway. Otherwise it's almost certainly best to stay where you are.

The only exception to this rule might be if you are trading up and can find a highly motivated seller. All property investors know that the day they make their profit is the day they buy well. In a property downturn there'll always be motivated sellers. Such an individual may:

- Have been repossessed
- Have a property that would be good to fix up but he can't now do it
- Be under serious pressure from his bank
- Have personal reasons for having to sell or

As long as you do your homework in exactly the way you would in a buoyant market, you could do well. Just because something appears cheap in the current market is no reason to get sloppy…in fact there's a greater chance of things going wrong at such a time, so you'll need to be even more cautious. I know it'll sound rather vulture-like but you'll need to hone your skills at finding opportunities. Get auction catalogues; get to know estate agents (they'll be grateful for a sale); talk to surveyors, architects and designers who'll have clients that have briefed them on projects they can longer afford; and so on.

Depending on how aggressive you want to be, you could actually go out into the marketplace looking for such opportunities. Local planning offices have details of all planning applications. Many will never get built in a recession. Perhaps you could do the current owner a favour and take their project over. Look for special properties that might not normally come up. A business going bust could provide an interesting property on which to get change of use and then make a home for yourself. Property-linked professionals of all kinds will have clients with properties to sell. The opportunities are limited only by your ingenuity and you'll discover just how much you have once you get your teeth into things.

Depending on where you believe things are in the property cycle, you could do well by moving before the actual bottom of the market if it means you'll be in a better position long-term by, for example, moving to a better area where, once the market improves, your gain will be greater than staying put in your current home. But this calls for cool nerves, as you may not be able to assess the market accurately.

The problem with buying now, though, is that you simply may not be able to get a mortgage if you need one, however good a bargain or opportunity your new place appears to be. Traditionally, bad times have provided good opportunities for those trading up. But things are very different today. The only exception to this is if you are in cash. With cash in hand, at the moment, you can do very well. Of course, you may choose to use this cash to invest in some other sort of asset rather than property.

Finally, be aware that sellers today won't actually decide to sell to you unless you can prove that you have the funds. If you are in a chain, expect to be treated rather cautiously. Also, bear in mind when you're working out your finances that you'll not only have to be able to afford to buy your new place but you'll also need to live.

Is it a good time to rent?

Yes, if it's you're first home (or for whatever other reason you have nothing to sell). There are several reasons I say this:

- It's best not to buy anything until the property market has settled down, or you could see your new home's value falling very quickly

- There are lots of properties to rent, as increasing numbers of those who bought buy-to-lets are falling on hard times and are pleased to have tenants, and even some holiday and second homes are being let. Deals can be done with those landlords who are struggling to pay their mortgages. The only small danger here is they might just go bad on you and you could find yourself out of a home. As a consolation, should this occur, there'll be many other opportunities out there

  Larger family homes are currently letting well but this could change as financial hardship bites. In the meantime there are thousands of cheaper, especially city-centre, flats and those that developers cannot sell that can be rented for a reasonable price

- Whatever the lenders claim (and they have, in public) it's still cheaper to rent in these circumstances than to buy. The costs of buying are so high that renting can win hands-down in the early years. It has been calculated that a £200,000 home will leave you about £23,000 worse off over your first year's occupation, compared with the cost of renting a similar place. Matters slightly improve over the next few years but not by that much! Don't forget that the cash you would have spent on a deposit and all the trimmings involved in buying could be invested and making you good money at a time when interest rates to savers are rising. If you are thinking of renting for many years, then buying is indeed a better bet financially

The bigger economic picture

The construction and house-building industries have played a huge role in the economic growth of many western countries in recent years. In the Republic of Ireland there was a time recently when one quarter of the entire economy revolved around the construction industry. In the US only a few years ago, nearly half of the increase in all private sector employment was accounted for by building.

The reason is easy to see. A house is only the tip of a vast iceberg of cash which generates jobs for estate agents, solicitors, mortgage brokers, accountants, the insurance industry, large-scale builders, furniture and home improvement companies, small builders, building suppliers of many kinds, lending institutions, and, of course, the Government. If you add up all the taxes involved in the production of a new house they come to about half its price! There's capital gains tax to be paid on the sale of the land to the builder; the builder creates jobs and his workers all pay income tax; the builder pays taxes on his profit; VAT is payable by all and sundry, yielding yet more tax; all the suppliers in the chain pay tax on their profits; the person buying the house has to earn the money (after paying tax) to pay for everything; the buyer also has to pay a purchase tax (stamp duty); and so on. When the housing market is buoyant and especially when house-building is brisk, the government makes loads of money in taxes. This cash can then be used to do what politicians have pledged to achieve. Or they can pay off some of the national debt. In really good times they can do both!

So when the property market is booming, the tax it

generates supports lots of things we all want. When the going gets tough, or when there's an actual recession in the market, governments simply can't afford to do what they would like, or we demand.

Over the past two decades or so, most of us have felt better off because our homes were rising in value, if only on paper. This gave us the confidence (well-placed or not) to borrow against our property and to spend more in general. In a consumer society, this drove the economy at large.

Now there's a downturn some people will go bankrupt, some will lose their jobs, others will lose their homes and some will not be able to buy a home at all. All this means that home ownership levels will fall, if only for a while. Opportunists and those who bought buy-to-lets in city centres where developers built for this market rather than for any real need for local housing, are among the first to feel the pain. Many of those who dabbled in the market have been the first to get out and their financial lives in general are struggling as a result.

At this stage of the downturn, smart money doesn't even consider investing in property, no-one sells unless they have to, and the market freezes for a while. Surprise and concern soon turn to panic and despair and the whole economy drifts into recession. Whether or not the Government officially defines this dire situation as a recession is somewhat academic to the home-owner who feels the very bottom has fallen out of his financial world and may also be worried about his job. In reality, we all have our very personal definition of the term 'recession'. The business group, the British Chambers of Commerce said, in August 2008, that it believed recession was 'inevitable'. So whatever any of us may personally think, perhaps the reality is closer than we'd dared imagine.

A leading economist has calculated that a 10% fall in house prices will cause the loss of 100 basis points off growth, largely because of the effect on our consumer-led economy. A 15% drop in prices would, he claims, send the economy into a true recession. Most significantly, the Governor of the Bank of England has ruled out anything that would mean the government getting into the mortgage market except by bailing out bankers.

In November 2008 the UK government reduced VAT from 17.5% to 15% for a period of 13 months, to try to stimulate the economy. Those of us who know the housing market cannot see this producing any meaningful positive results on the home-ownership front.

More than four million households have had to turn to credit cards or personal loans to cover their mortgage or rent payments in 2008. This servicing of long-term debt with short-term, expensive, borrowing is a time-bomb in itself. Apart from the fact that taking out a personal loan to service long-term debt while pretending it is for something else, is legally fraud! In this situation, those who have savings, preferably in cash, come out best. This makes situations like this a good opportunity to re-assess your values and priorities. The observed facts are that at these times, those with deep pockets survive and even thrive whilst those who are working close to their financial limits do badly. Whether or not most of us will learn much from these tough lessons, and apply them for the future, only time will tell. If experience from the 1990s recession is anything to go by, I don't think we will.

For example, a poll carried out for the BBC in 2008 found that, in spite of seeing what's happening now, 81% of those asked said they wanted the value of their homes to rise!

While thinking of the illiquidity of property in general, but especially in a downturn, it might be helpful to say something about stocks and shares. People often talk of spreading their investments over various types of asset. And this makes sense. But whereas when we buy shares we know full-well that their value could fall, most of us hoped, until recently, that property assets could only rise in value, or at best stand still. This means that when the going gets tough, most property owners stick in there and wait for what they've always seen to be the inevitable better times ahead. Nobody ever thinks this way about, for example, shares in the plastics industry. Stock markets can fluctuate massively and very quickly as people panic buy or sell. This cannot happen in property, if only because houses are so slow and expensive to get rid of, even when times are good.

But other factors come into play too. For most of us our homes aren't just 'investments', however we may fool ourselves – they are places to live, sources of personal fulfilment and satisfaction, physical locations that set us within our community, and are perceived, if anything, to be more like consumer goods rather than stocks and shares. I looked on page 23 at one reason why the British seem to get such a rush out of investing so much time and money on their homes and obvious status is certainly a real motive. If you have millions of gold mine shares, no one knows, or even much cares. But if you have a beautiful home it is plain for everyone to see. In an increasingly shallow and showy world that reveres open demonstrations of wealth and 'celebrity', this will change only if our underlying thinking and values change.

Perhaps the housing downturn in association with climate change and other serious world-wide economic issues, might trigger this.

Rented accommodation

We have seen that just over seventy per cent of people own their home in the UK. This leaves more than a quarter who do not. There are three main sources of rented accommodation: private landlords, local councils, and housing associations. About eleven percent of people rent their home through a private landlord and the rest through some sort of public (social) housing. Within social housing, just over two million households rent from local authorities and just under two million from housing associations.

The term 'social housing' is rather unfortunate and even harks back to the days of the work-house in the minds of older people. This said, millions of people happily live a whole life-time in rented homes that are not provided by the private sector. With the growth of housing associations (see below) there's now a source of high-quality 'social' housing that can match anything in the private sector. This is removing the old British stigma of 'council housing' that has plagued the public rental market for generations.

Private rentals

There are three main private sources of rental properties. Corporations (largely involved with the top end of the market in large cities); individual landlords (who have anything from a single property to a small bank of housing units to let); and private individuals with a single, surplus house (often inherited, unused while they're abroad, or un-needed by a family member) that they want to keep but not live in.

This picture has changed over the last year or two as some home-owners have become what has been called 'accidental landlords'. According to the Royal Institution of Chartered Surveyors, the numbers of privately-owned properties available to rent has risen faster than at any time since records began a decade ago. With agents selling on average only one property a week, thousands of those who'd planned to sell cannot do so and are letting their homes instead. But becoming a landlord brings responsibilities and duties, as well as some welcome cash. The National Landlords Association has pointed out that these 'accidental landlords' should do their homework very carefully or they could fall foul of things such as tenancy deposit protection; gas and fire safety certificates; and tenant references. For helpful information see www.landlords.org.uk

Whilst more than 70% of households today own their own homes, as we've seen, at the turn of the twentieth century most people rented. This continued until the start of the mass housing-for-sale market in the early 1930s. At this stage, landlordism wasn't the best profession to be in from a social standing point of view. This said, large numbers of the aristocracy and the middle class owned properties that they rented out. Many were good landlords but some were not.

Over the years after World War II, successive governments started to impose controls on private rented property, both to fix rents and to introduce minimum housing standards so people didn't find themselves living in slums.

All this made letting homes harder and less financially attractive for landlords, who, as a result, started to retreat from rental housing as an investment. The Rachman scandal put the final nail in the coffin in the early 1960s. Peter Rachman was a London landlord in the 1950s and '60s who ran a rental housing empire. His rents were often high and the condition of his properties low and he became infamous for his ruthless treatment of those who didn't pay their rent. The term 'Rachmanism' was coined to describe landlords who behaved in the same way. His methods gave landlords a bad name and undoubtedly led many concerned people to desert the business.

House prices were by now rising and renting became less financially and socially attractive to investors, so most private landlords sold up.

The next major milestone in private rented housing was the sudden popularity of buy-to-let properties. The seeds of this trend were sown soon after the Housing Act of 1988, when the concept of Assured Freehold Tenants meant that people could rent for a minimum period of six months and landlords could be guaranteed vacant possession. By about 1999, large numbers of people, who had never considered themselves landlords, started to buy the odd single property as an investment to let out. The huge rises in capital value of these properties were the main attraction, and in a booming market many people did indeed see considerable gains. Some ambitious individuals bought small banks of properties with easily-available, cheap money, and became a new breed of landlord. In mid-2008 there were about one million buy-to-let properties in the UK.

In the nineties developers started building for this market, based on increasingly attractive returns for investors. All this newly-created housing was for short-term rental, largely aimed at first-time buyers, young professionals, students and so on. The buy-to-let phenomenon arose because money was easy to come by and ordinary people could borrow cash, perhaps against their own home's inflated value, to play the game. And they came from far and wide to do so. Many buy-to-lets were bought by

Chinese, Indian, and Irish investors who couldn't bear to miss out on the 'next big thing' in the UK property market.

Unfortunately, as with so many 'money-spinners' in life, buy-to-lets weren't founded on reality. Many developers built just for this market and, as a result, far too many dwellings were built – particularly in the last decade – in places where people didn't actually want to live or, at least, not in such numbers. It soon became apparent that in some, especially city-centre areas, there were simply too many flats in the buy-to-let market and when money started tightening up, there were too few investors and too few tenants. As there was no real local market for these properties, they became unsellable. This is the state of affairs at the time of writing. Many small investors, thinking they were on to a sure thing, have in fact lost money – some, small fortunes.

Between 1998 and 2007, buy-to-let mortgages rose from £2 billion to £120 billion. But there are signs that things are about to change dramatically, according to a study by Skandia. They have estimated that the value of these mortgages will fall from today's £120 billion to £44 billion over the next few years as investors sell around two thirds of their properties, in the face of falling prices. After all, these investors went into the business to make money. Many of them now realise that to preserve their wealth, they'll need to look outside the property market.

Large investors from other countries tend to take a much longer view of their property portfolios and will stick in there for twenty or more years. Many, if not most, ordinary buy-to-letters in the UK went in for a fast buck. Sadly for them they ignored the first principle of property investment – that it is, by definition, a long-term affair.

Renting from a private landlord

Today, if you see renting as a second-class way of providing yourself with a roof, I'd strongly advise you to abandon the notion. Of course, if the property market is booming it can seem unwise to rent if you could buy for much the same money each month but today's market makes this a poor choice. And this looks like being the case for some years to come. People everywhere claim that renting is a way of pouring money down the drain but we all need a roof over our heads and this costs money. When house prices are static or falling it's a great time to invest any money you have and to rent someone else's property. As I've pointed out in Chapter Three, millions of continentals rent for a whole lifetime and use their remaining cash to live. But this attitude is alien to many British who have, for many decades, seen their home as a win-win investment and renting to be a poor person's alternative. As the realities of the property market bite, the investment argument no longer holds water.

Renting is essential for those of us who can't afford to buy and can also be ideal for the many of us who could buy but are looking for something relatively short-term, or who'd rather use our capital for something other than housing. Most of us in the UK start off renting while saving for a deposit to buy somewhere but this will now change as more people rent on a more permanent basis as a positive lifestyle choice, rather than a second-best one.

When choosing a home to rent, you're in exactly the same position, in many ways, as if you were going to buy. You have to find the right home and be able to pay for it.

Looking around. Once you've decided on your area, get out there and do the homework. Walk around to get a feel of the neighbourhood and then go to estate agents, look in local papers, surf the web (for example, www.findaproperty.com), look on newsagents' boards and generally keep your eyes and ears open for opportunities. Other helpful websites are www.loot.co.uk and www.gumtree.com. In general, the market is over-supplied with smaller units (such as one- and two-bed flats) and under-supplied with larger family homes. This could change in the future as we alter our attitudes to renting on a more permanent basis.

At this stage it's important to consider how long you might be renting and what you think the property market is doing, if you intend, eventually, to buy. If you are looking for a home for several years your needs will be different from if you are looking for a one-year tenancy pending a move somewhere for work, for example. If your intentions are long-term you'll need to do all your homework on schools, local facilities and so on, just as if you were buying. The difference now, though, is that you won't be looking at all this with a view to a property's capital-growth potential, but simply as a family wanting to live somewhere – and make a home for yourselves.

View with care. Even if you are thinking of only a short-term rent, be sure to view potential properties carefully. Life can be hell within a week if you make a bad choice. Make sure the place has all the facilities you need and that it appears to be in good order. According to the level of the market you're looking at you'll be able to be more or less picky. Think what really matters to you and check as you go round that the place fits the bill. Be especially careful about neighbours. Look out for rubbish in common parts; judge how annoying other people's bikes or baby buggies will be, stuck in the entrance hall; try to assess how noisy it'll be;

look at the outdoor areas, and so on. It can be hard to take all this in when you're there for only a few minutes, so if in any doubt, go back for a second look and take your partner or a friend for a second opinion. It amazes agents and landlords how little research most tenants do before renting somewhere. This is usually far less than when buying yet it can end up in a very expensive mistake.

Dealing with the agent. Letting agencies are just like other types of estate agency. They list properties and make money by charging the landlord a commission on the rental they obtain for him. Clearly, it's in the agent's best interests to get the most rent he can but you'll need to negotiate this to your best advantage. When rental properties are relatively scarce, as can occur in a poor housing market when many more people are looking to rent, this can be hard. At the time of writing, rents are rising because of a relatively poor supply of properties where people want them. Look at what else is available in the local rental market and, if necessary, get someone to share with you to make the whole thing more affordable. This said, it's still good to haggle, especially when the cost of living is rising and you could be grateful for a little extra each month towards paying some bills. You'll be in a strong position to do a deal if the type of property you're looking for is in over-supply. At the time of going to press, rentals were falling on city-centre blocks of flats.

Agents will charge you fees for some of their work: for example, for getting a credit reference or other references on you. Ask the agent what he'll be charging you, as opposed to billing the landlord.

Check the inventory. I can't stress enough how important this is. I've rented homes and been a landlord and know how vital this is from everyone's point of view. Go through the whole list very carefully and also note (with photos, dated and copied to the agent) anything in the place that isn't in perfect order. For example, take pictures of any scuffed paintwork, damage, and so on. This will be your evidence of how the place was when you took it over. If there are things that need doing before you start your tenancy, now is the time to say so. Most landlords will be on their best behaviour at this time and eager to please. I always check that machines work; that all windows and doors open and shut properly; that the water-heating functions as it should; and so on. Check too that there is a current, gas safety certificate and that the property passes the required fire safety regulations – the agent should know about this.

Put in writing anything that worries you, so it's there from the start. Most landlords are fair and decent and may not even be aware of the problems. When I let anything, I go round making sure it's exactly how I'd like to live. Many landlords don't do this. This said, having been told that, say, the washing machine doesn't work, most will take care of the matter quickly. In one way, anything you tell your landlord should be welcomed as he'll be pleased that you are concerned about his investment. When I am renting from a landlord I always take the view that if the place were mine I'd like to be told when things were going wrong.

Money and contracts. Having agreed on the rent you'll pay you'll now need a contract. The most common one used in the private sector is a 'shorthold tenancy'. In this you agree to take the place for a certain length of time (the 'term'). This will start with an initial six-month minimum period but you can agree on any number of months, or even years, beyond this. A rental contract should tell you the date the tenancy began; the amount of rent payable and the dates when it is due; how the rent will be reviewed; how long the agreement lasts for; and how much notice you need to give should you want to leave (should be a minimum of two months). In addition there could be all manner of other issues in the contract, from any annual maintenance charge to how you dry your laundry and whether or not you can keep a dog!

If you have any doubts about your contract, take advice from a solicitor or a local advice centre.

Your landlord will usually want you to pay some rent – often a month's – in advance and also a deposit, possibly of a similar amount, so he has some cash in hand should he need to make repairs etc if you damage something. If you leave the place as you found it (apart from 'fair wear and tear') you'll get this 'holding deposit' back in full. Unfortunately, it is not at all uncommon for landlords to hold on to this deposit for longer than they should, or even to dispute how much should be deducted for work that needs doing. This can be a stressful time. Be persistent and you'll get a result eventually. There are now Tenancy Deposit Schemes that should protect you. Talk to the agent about this. If your income should fall dramatically, or you become unemployed, you could be eligible for Local Housing Allowance. For details, see www.direct.gov.uk or ask your local council's housing advice centre.

Social housing

All but a very small number of people in a country like Britain are housed one way or another. I look at the homeless below. Even people with very little or no income can have a home, thanks to Housing Benefits (for details, see www.direct.gov.uk). But in between those who can afford to rent privately in the open market and those who can't, is a large number of individuals and families who still need to be housed.

This large group includes many surprising people such as nurses, teachers, firemen, the low-paid who run our local government services, many of the elderly, some of those who are mentally ill or disabled and can't hold down a job, and many others. Such people may not be 'poor' but they still can't afford to pay a commercial private rent. They are housed in some form of social housing. There are about 4.5 million such tenancies today in England, which are supplied by several different sources.

Over the centuries, various *benefactors, trusts* and *charities* have provided housing for the poor. Giant organisations such as the Peabody Trust and the Guinness Trust still have huge holdings today. Millions of people over the years have had reason to be grateful to the beneficent founding fathers of these charities.

Some local councils still retain true *'council properties'* as in times gone by, and it has to be said that certain councils are better housing managers than are some housing trusts (see below); but the majority of social, rented housing today is provided by some sort of a body that is rather different from the local council.

In the late 1980s *Tenant Management Organisations* (TMOs) were set up and the government launched so-called Arm's Length Management Organisations (ALMOs) where the councils still own their housing stock but empower a management company to run things. As the committees included tenants, matters improved very quickly and the system was very successful. Some ALMOs have worked wonders in cities such as Derby, the Kensington and Chelsea area of London, Hounslow, and Sheffield, and many of the best ALMOs are chaired by a tenant.

But by far the biggest change in the social housing scene came with the growth of the housing associations in the 1930s, followed by their larger development in the 1970s.

Housing associations

These are not-for-profit companies (often known today as Registered Social Landlords – RSLs), or trusts that provide low-cost housing for people who cannot afford to buy or rent in the main market. All profits from sales, or rental income, are used to build further homes and to maintain existing ones. Housing associations now create more rental homes than do any other sector in the UK. It is also possible to buy a share of a home from such associations (and then pay rent on the remaining proportion of its value), in a 'shared ownership' scheme: but the majority in housing association schemes rent.

The National Housing Federation has about 1,400 member organisations that provide two million social housing units over the whole of England. These currently house around five million people.

Both local authorities and central government fund housing associations by way of grants. And, as I've already mentioned, they have incomes from rentals. One major housing association has a rental income of £80 million a year. The sums involved are impressive. Housing associations, between 2006 and 2008, delivered more than 80,000 new social homes, supplementing more than £4 billion of public grant with £3 billion of private borrowings and a further £3 billion from their own reserves and property sales. In 2007 they also spent more than £1.8 billion maintaining and repairing their housing stock. In addition to this, housing associations invest millions each year in neighbourhood services.

In general, housing association rents are about half those of the private market for a comparable home.

Housing associations also, of course, need to borrow money to build new homes and to buy land. This puts them at the mercy of the normal property and finance markets to some extent, so they have to be commercially smart as well as being non-profit-making. This said, a housing association is a good bet for a lender as there is a lot of equity and a guaranteed income stream. Perhaps I should mention here that council and housing association tenants are brilliant payers. The default rate is much lower than in the private rental sector!

The big growth in housing associations came about in the 1970s and '80s when legalisation changed to make it impossible for local councils to subsidise their council housing from local taxes; and forced them to put all their government grant money for new homes through housing associations. Several other things also changed. Local councils started cutting costs, and the introduction of housing benefits schemes that favoured housing associations rather than local authorities meant that many councils began to transfer their housing stock to housing associations. This transfer wasn't universal, though, and today there are still some homes owned by local authorities.

Before 1974, about eighty per cent of all social housing was owned by councils. Today this figure is about fifty per cent. However, this is a national figure that masks the reality that in some areas there is no local authority housing at all. Before a council could transfer it's housing stock, tenants were asked whether they'd rather be part of a local council housing scheme or a housing association. The vast majority opted for the latter. They then became part of the board or committee that ran the place and this raised standards and made people feel more responsible for and involved in their living environment. It is impossible today to distinguish many housing association estates from privately-owned ones, so high is their quality of build and their level of upkeep.

Housing associations are managed by paid staff, watched over by a management committee, or board, generally made up of volunteers. This board has the overall responsibility for the running of each association. Such management structures can be very small or huge. One major London housing association has a full-time paid staff of more than 200 people and manages half a billion pounds worth of rental property.

Housing associations provide a whole range of different types of housing from small groups of about 12 homes in rural areas, to massive estates in city centres. Much of the 'supported housing' in the UK is also provided by housing associations and some have special accommodation specifically for the homeless, the mentally ill, the elderly, or even substance abusers.

Housing associations buy land, or may even be given land, and build from scratch, or they can get housing built for them by a developer who is already creating a development of private homes. Under a planning arrangement called a Section 106 Agreement, a developer may be given planning permission by the local authority to do what he wants, provided he creates an agreed number of new, affordable, homes as part of his plan. The developer then sells off these affordable homes to a housing association and the association manages them. The builder still makes a sensible (though reduced) profit, so this isn't a charity job of any kind. And why should it be?

Such affordable housing cannot usually be bought on the open market in the normal way but is accessed via the council's housing lists (see page 90). These homes are usually made available to key workers (nurses, doctors, firemen, policemen, etc) who live in the area. The sad irony is that there's too little joined-up thinking in the matter of housing key workers. For example, in London, a police-owned site was sold off to the private sector when it should have been developed for much-needed police housing. Similarly, school playing fields are being sold off, yet the schools' own teachers often cannot afford to buy locally and have long commutes. This type of silliness occurs all too frequently – unfortunately. Alas, it will continue unless theres more joined-up thinking.

It's a pity that the supply of section 106 homes is already starting to dry up as developers, under huge financial pressure, are shutting down sites and not starting new ones. Given that this valuable source of social housing rides on the back of the private sector's developments, it's easy to see that this will cease until the market improves and developers start to build again.

Shared ownership

Affordable housing is not, however, all that cheap. This means that most people will end up buying only a fraction of their place and paying rent on the rest. This is known as 'shared ownership'. The government's shared ownership scheme is called New Build Home Buy. It is aimed largely at helping key workers find housing in their area. Your local HomeBuy agent at your local council offices will tell you if your occupation is considered to be a 'key' one in your area. If it is, you can buy your home outright within five years but you have to sell it to someone the housing association approves of, or back to them. When working out what percentage you can afford to buy, don't forget service charges and other expenses.

Shared ownership might be the only way you can get a home at all. You can buy a share from 25% up to 75% and it's possible to increase the amount you buy over the years. Each housing association differs on its policies on this.

The down-sides are that there can be a long wait; your choice will be limited; you may have to pay for maintenance costs; you'll need permission to make alterations; and you'll probably never be able to buy the whole of your home in some areas. If you're thinking of going this route, talk to a solicitor who knows the (many) questions that will need answering, and in particular what happens when you want to move and sell your share of the property.

I mentioned Section 106 agreements above. As well as providing 'affordable' homes, a developer may be required to build some 'social' housing too. This will be entirely for rent and will be accessed via the council's housing list for those who cannot afford to buy even a share of their home. Their numbers will be rising over the coming years.

But although I may have made things sound great in the social rental world, and indeed things are better than they were, there's a terrible shortage of social housing. Studies done by The National Housing Federation show that:

- Housing lists have grown by 57% in the last five years, to more than 1.7 million households
- These lists now involve nearly four million people
- Nearly 100,000 further homeless households are living in temporarily accommodation, including 4,000 households in bed and breakfast hotels
- Council and housing association homes have fallen in number by one third since 2001
- Only one third of all local authorities have seen any rise in their social housing stock since 2001
- There is a need for 70,000 new social homes every year to keep up with demand

Getting access to social housing

To get any sort of social housing you need to go through your local council's housing department. They have a housing list. This is widely known as the 'waiting list' but should really be called the 'weighting list' because it has little to do with time, which is what people think, but more to do with points (weightings) that put you nearer, or further away from, the top of the list. Anyone can put their name on the waiting list. And all local authorities must, by law, keep a list.

One in 13 households in England and Wales is on such a list!

Every year, each council trawls its list and cuts it down to those who are most eligible. Housing need is assessed according to many factors that have been tried and tested over the years. Is the family over-crowded? Do they have an elderly, dependent person living with them? Have they children? If so, what ages are they? Is the applicant mentally or physically ill? And so on. If you want to see how to get on to your local authority's waiting list, go to their website or their advice centre.

When looking for public housing to rent, or if you fear you're about to lose your home, you should use the council as your starting point. The council is the 'strategic housing authority' that allocates homes from their own stock or those run by housing associations. The first place to go is your local authority's housing advice centre. Here, specialists will listen carefully to your situation. They know the area's housing intimately, even down to individual landlords and private developments and they often have lists of private homes for rent. Although such facilities might appear rather 'socialist', the very first one in London was established by John Major, a Tory councillor for housing in 1975, who later became prime minister. If you'd rather go to a citizen's advice bureau, they will also help you get started on this complex journey.

Every council has a Strategic Housing Plan and a Letting Plan within it. A council's lettings manager administers this letting plan on a day-by-day basis. Since 1972, councillors haven't been allowed to be involved in this process. This keeps everything above board. Time was when all kinds of professionals, from councillors to doctors and lawyers, would try to influence things to get their particular candidate a council house. This is all much clearer now and has made things a lot fairer.

When allocating housing, local authority housing officers try to create a social mix that represents the community as a whole within any one area or estate. This means that there should be no undue excess of any one section of the community. However, social housing is in limited supply, so the task of juggling what's available and matching this with those who want it, can leave some people disappointed. If you don't get offered what you'd like, you'll have to wait, or reduce your aspirations. On balance, it's always wise to accept what you're offered or you might come across as picky and put yourself at a disadvantage. As your life situation changes (for example, you have opposite-sex children over the age of twelve who need separate bedrooms, or your health changes for the worse), you can apply for something else.

If you're in a council house (rather than a housing association home) you have the right to buy at a discount. Rent-to-buy schemes are being talked about and these make a lot of sense. Here you would pay rent in the normal way but have some of this total rental you've paid taken off the price, should you decide to buy.

Of those on a council's waiting list (looked at nationally), about 50% get a housing association place and the other 50% a council house. This proportion varies from council to council, of course, because in some areas there are almost no council houses to rent. Each local authority has its strategic plan that clarifies exactly how many people they can house in any given year. They know how many homes are coming on stream, and so on. The main problem is dealing with big families, as there aren't enough large properties for them. The majority of people in social housing are elderly and there are also specific sheltered housing schemes that can help them in particular ways.

A group of people for whom local authorities have special responsibility are the 'statutory homeless'. These are people who have lost their home as a result of a fire, flood or other tragedy beyond their control, or because they've been threatened with repossession and have nowhere else to live. The homeless person's unit at your local authority has highly specialist officers who can arrange for emergency accommodation in such a crisis. These officers will go through your life history and assess your situation. On occasion they can even help you fight your landlord threatening you with eviction, as their primary task is to prevent homelessness. Such experts can also put you on to a law centre, which can get you legal aid, or whatever is necessary.

While they look into everything, you'll be offered somewhere temporary to live. Initially this could be Bed and Breakfast accommodation. Or you could be offered a temporary, leased property (for example, a one- or two-bed flat). You can stay in this until you get a permanent offer. It's wise to go with what you're offered, as you may not get another offer. The majority of those who find themselves in this situation, get a job, find other accommodation, and get back on their feet before long.

At any one time there are around 100,000 statutory homeless in the UK (60% of whom are in London). Don't be afraid to go to a homeless unit. Allow the system to help you.

Homelessness

It is estimated that there are about 800,000 homeless (as opposed to statutory homeless, see above) people in the UK, of whom about half are 'hidden'.

Those of us with a home rarely consider those without one. I became interested when working as a volunteer for CRISIS, the homeless charity. Frankly, it is impossible to have a life-long interest in housing and not be compelled to consider and have compassion for, homeless people. The hours I spent listening helped me put my fascination with housing into a different perspective and changed me for ever. The truth is that once you don't have a home, other things can very quickly start to go wrong in your life. Perfectly capable and intelligent individuals soon find themselves enmeshed in a complicated lifestyle in which one disadvantage reinforces another, spiralling them downwards.

People become homeless for various reasons, most of which don't make them into the 'wasters' so many housed people imagine. The most common reason is that friends and family can no longer house them and they have nowhere else to go.

The breakdown of relationships is also a very common cause, accounting for nearly one fifth of the homeless. Domestic violence; those leaving home or care; people coming out of hospitals, the armed forces or prison; the death of a partner; and debt (mortgage and rent arrears or even repossession) account for the rest. As a relationships therapist for twenty years I am, understandably, most interested in this second-largest group. It was an intensely humbling experience, reminding myself continually that, 'There but for the grace of God, go I'.

Many people have asked me whether the homeless choose their lifestyle. I don't know the facts and figures and probably no one really does, but I'd say it's only a tiny minority that make this way of life a conscious choice. Some homeless people I met – especially the 'rough sleepers ' – certainly said they felt better out of doors rather than being 'tied down' by living in bricks and mortar, but they were a minority.

Homeless people largely live in:

- Bed and Breakfast accommodation
- Hostels, Night Shelters and Refuges
- Accommodation provided by friends or family. Clearly, such people live on the 'charity' of those giving them a roof. They have no rights and can be thrown out at a moment's notice.
- Squats (about 10,000 people at any one time)

A book such as this is no place to look at the ins and outs of homelessness but the subject will be of interest to some readers who, with the repossession of their home, could become homeless, perhaps for the first time. There's little doubt that as the housing crisis deepens, more people will find themselves in this life-changing predicament than ever would have thought possible. If this looks even a remote possibility, seek help from a Citizen's Advice Bureau.

For more information, also see www.crisis.org.uk

Eco-towns

The UK government has deemed that the country is short of about three million homes, or will be so by 2020. One answer to this shortage is to create a number of new towns in the countryside throughout the land. At the time of writing, 15 potential sites have been established and about half of these will eventually end up being built, after consultation with many interested parties, both national and local.

In principle these towns will have a population of up to 20,000 each, though some will be only a quarter this size, and be constructed to the very best of sustainable, green, building methods, with best-practice water conservation systems, state-of-the-art recycling and wonderful public transport. It is also proposed that such new towns would have to have at least 30-50% social housing (see page 89 to create homes for key workers and others who cannot afford to buy even so–called 'affordable' housing.

The Government has asked private sector companies to bid for these sites. Their proposals will then be debated in public and decisions made very quickly.

Sounds a good idea?
At first, yes....but:

Cars

Unfortunately, some of the proposed sites are government-owned properties that are way out in the countryside. This would involve future inhabitants in long car journeys at a time when fuel prices are at their highest ever and people are already avoiding car journeys whenever they can. If low-cost, green public transport could answer most people's needs for local journeys this could be a good start but it'll be unlikely to allay the fears of many future inhabitants. Car clubs, for example, have been tried elsewhere on small developments and found to work but whether they would do so on a scale such as this has never been tested.

The locals

Existing local rural communities are, understandably, concerned that 'their' countryside will become an urban, or at best suburban, mess, with many such protesters claiming they're not against new housing per se but that they don't think the middle of the countryside is the right place for it. Many housing experts feel this is a fair criticism, looked at dispassionately. There's a good case for building such new housing alongside existing communities, perhaps by expanding suburban areas where facilities already exist and where public transport can easily be extended to serve the new population.

Of course, such rural dwellers' protestations immediately raise cries of 'nimbyism', and even of class battles for which the British are well known. It is easy to see the argument that 'posh' people living in rural bliss don't want the 'great unwashed' on their doorstep with all their pollution, crime, noise, traffic, litter and so on.

Planning matters

In many of the proposed areas, local planning policy wouldn't allow such schemes at all. This is being overcome by the government altering planning law in ways we could all later regret. In 2004, the government gave the power to decide on housing numbers to easily-controlled regional assemblies, thus disempowering county councils. Further planning changes are going through which will hand regional development agencies power and control over housing. Given that these bodies will be largely bent on economic development, it's easy to see how they might view housing. All these changes and the government's overt backing for eco-towns are making locals and others doubt that they'll be opposed in any meaningful way at planning. If they go to appeal, the government will push them through.

No finance

The next issue that could bring the eco-town idyll to its knees is the shortage of builders and developers who'll be willing to take the job on. When they were first asked to show their hand, about 60 developers were keen. But that was before the realities of the credit crunch. Such outfits would now be very hard-pushed to find the funds, and the developers who'd be expected to make things happen on the ground have so much unsold stock of their own that they'll be unlikely, over the next few years, to build yet more homes that will compete with theirs. It simply won't happen. And who can blame them? Many such companies are fighting for their financial and corporate lives. I can't see them embracing this adventure with any enthusiasm for some time to come.

No builders

For the next few years, and possibly even for many more beyond, the shortage of tradesmen is going to prove a stumbling block to building anything like the numbers of homes the government wants, be they green or any other colour. The Olympic sites are short of skilled workmen and even once the great games are out of our hair, and assuming the government has any money left – its coffers shrunk from reduced fuel, income and property taxes – there's no evidence there'll be enough people to build these homes. Don't forget, the eco-towns are only a small part of a much bigger government-inspired building project – to create millions of new homes. As I know from my experience in the building world, many eastern Europeans are going – or have already gone – home. Having made good money they understandably want to live in Poland, Latvia, Estonia or Lithuania among friends and family in their familiar culture rather than in Britain. On a recent trip to a building corporation in Estonia I was struck by how many tradesmen had gone back, now their own country is a better place to live, and with cash in their pockets to buy somewhere nice for themselves and their families. Wage levels too are falling (relative to the cost of living) in the UK and back home their euro goes a lot further. The Promised Land is no longer the Republic of Ireland or Britain.

No experience

It's a very long time since anyone in the UK built a new town. Most of the originals are at least a generation old. Lessons learned have, of course, been well documented but that's no substitute for skilled professionals who know how to do it. And they've all retired. It's easy to build a neighbourhood but it's vastly more difficult to build a community. It would be foolish to assume that mass market builders can do anything other than create buildings and neighbourhoods – at best. They don't claim to be town planners or urban lifestyle experts, let alone to know how to plan for education, leisure, culture, the elderly, young families, transport, industry and all kinds of other essentials that make a living town work. All this will mean people at every level learning on the job and trying to get it right. Just ask yourself what the chances are of such 'prototype' towns ever being what people really enjoy living in. Given all this, and people's experience of such 'new towns' as we've already had in the UK, it's easy to feel pretty depressed about it all. It would be great to think that a new generation of aware, young urban planners would do better than their forefathers but I can't think it'll be a lot better.

Not eco

A few years ago my architect partner and I were approached by a developer to plan a green village. It wasn't easy to do. Large architectural practices are now hell-bent on doing just this in various countries around the world, including China. But that's not in the UK! What most of us fear is that many so-called eco-towns will end up much the same as current, unimaginative, mass-market housing geared to the lowest common dominator while genuflecting to their, alleged, green credentials. The minute such projects are developer-led they have to be profitable first and foremost and as I know, from my own experience, it's hard to make really green communities and good profits. Add to this the government's desire for such a large proportion of, in effect, subsidised public housing, and the formula looks bleak. The Eco-towns Challenge Panel set up by the government to look at the proposals has found failings all over the place.

No money

The way things look at the moment, people can't even afford to buy normal, cheaply-produced, decidedly un-green, un-sustainable housing. As money gets tighter, with rising oil prices and everything that stems from them, it's entirely possible that over the next decade people will say, 'For God's sake give me a roof over my head and stuff how green it is.' We may not, as a nation, be able to afford the luxury of sustainable or green construction, whatever the gurus think. There's certainly an argument that modern construction, especially in the commercial world, cannot be sustained at its current high-carbon level but this doesn't apply to normal family homes that are light on concrete and steel. It would certainly be possible to improve green building methods to be less expensive than they are today but this won't happen soon and the savings won't be that great. One of the key facts about green and sustainable buildings is that, they cost more up-front, whatever their long-term, proven benefits. Cheap, mass-market housing is inexpensive to build exactly because it is not made from environmentally-friendly, green, or sustainable materials.

Eco-ghettos

My last concern is even more worrying than the rest. I fear that once such eco-towns are on the map they'll become ghettos rather than beacons. Of course such towns could, and should, become models of best practice that will be taken up by all new-builders. I hope this will happen but I doubt it. The more likely scenario is that builders and developers will look at what's been done and largely avoid it. Bill Dunster's revolutionary BedZed development in South London was a milestone. Yet nine years later have we seen dozens of similar projects sprouting from his creativity? We have not. Of course the world is changing and the green agenda is with us even more emphatically, given the climate change debate, but I won't be holding my breath.

Chapter 5
SELLING YOUR HOME

Although you may be able to avoid selling your home by one or more of the ways I look at on page 147, the time may come when you'll choose to, or need to, get out.

Very obviously (and I consider the subject in more detail on page 70), this is not the best time to sell either your home, or even an investment property, unless you really have to. Buyers will assume you're selling out of need rather than choice and will treat you and your property accordingly. They will do this knowing that there are more than one million unsold homes on the market in late-2008. As I write this, it is taking an average of 93 days to sell a property – one year ago this figure was 71 days. And this is for those properties that do sell! By the time this book is in the shops, this time-to-sell will be even longer.

If you find yourself in serious mortgage arrears, perhaps combined with other debts, you may *have* to sell to get yourself out of trouble. Bear in mind that if you are already in negative equity you'll need to get your lender's permission before selling.

Even once you've decided to sell it helps if you can continue servicing your mortgage while finding that buyer. This creates goodwill with your lender who can at least see you are doing your best. If you just let matters slip, for what could be many many, months in a poor market, they could, at worst, take you to court.

If you have an endowment or ISA mortgage you might be able to get your lender to allow you to pay less, thus reducing your monthly repayment. You may also be able to sell your investment or switch to a different type of mortgage. Talk to your lender or a mortgage broker about all this before panicking into selling up.

Some lenders will give you a mortgage interest holiday (or allow you to pay less by way of interest) if you are in financial difficulties and are trying to sell. All these routes are complicated and it's important to take financial advice. A book such as this can't hope to be sufficiently up to date in a fast-changing property market. There's no substitute for current professional advice. And, frankly, even very competent professionals are finding it hard to keep up with the ever-changing financial scene.

There are a few well-recognised steps involved in selling a property, whatever the market conditions. These become more or less important in a market in which the average estate agent is selling only one property a week.

Getting your property valued

I'd be very surprised if you had a realistic idea of what your home is worth in the current market. But if you are intending to sell to free yourself from financial problems you'll have to be very realistic about what you'll actually get for it. Otherwise you could be living in a fool's paradise when trying to work out how to pay off your debts and what, if anything, you can afford to buy when you move.

Who you get to do this valuation is up to you. The best person is a chartered surveyor as he'll have years of training, will also have professional insurance, and will be in touch with *values* rather than *prices* (as an estate agent might). But of course he will charge for his services. Many surveyors are also estate agents, so you could get the best of both worlds. Surveyors are also in touch with lending institutions (they do surveys for them) and can thus provide a good inside track into what lenders are thinking in this tricky market.

At the moment, valuers acting on behalf of lenders are being very harsh (realistic) about property values. This caution on behalf of the lenders for whom they are valuing, can knock substantial amounts off the value of your home. And you may already have reduced its price to sell, anyway. This might at first appear to be good news for buyers as it means prices will be lower but in reality it can mean their having to pay a bigger deposit as well as a higher interest rate as lenders take a cautious view. This phenomenon is also hitting those who are re-mortgaging to get themselves out of trouble. If you have only a small amount of equity, you could find yourself seeing this drained by a low valuation which, in turn, makes lenders ask for higher interest rates as there's suddenly not much of your own money in the place. This can be a terrible bind, though you may be able to pass on some of *your* lost value to others in the chain behind you.

If, despite your home's value being lower than you thought, you discover you have more value in your home than your mortgage (a difference known as your 'equity'), your lender will take a more relaxed view about how long it takes you to sell. If your home's value is less than what you owe, you'll be in 'negative equity'. At the time of writing, about half a million UK home-owners are in negative equity.

The Bank of England has calculated that this figure could rise to 1.2 million by 2011. Given that people tend to over-value their homes and under-value their debts, this figure could be over-optimistic. Perhaps the true figure is nearer three million.

Even once your home is sold (for less money than your mortgage) you'll still have to repay your lender in full. If you took out a mortgage indemnity guarantee when you bought, this should pay off the debt. But this money goes from the insurance company direct to your lender and you'll still have to pay off the original loan.

If the place you are selling in distress isn't your home (if it's an investment property, or a buy-to-let, for example), don't forget to allow for any capital gains tax you may have to pay. Talk to your accountant before you put it on the market.

If your lender shows signs of wanting to repossess your home, get an adviser (a solicitor, local housing advice centre, or Citizen's Advice Bureau), to talk to them on your behalf. Repossession and subsequent sale at auction may not secure the best price for your home, and your lender will know this.

It could be in their best interests to let you sell privately, provided this doesn't take too long. This could, though, all be taken out of your hands if your lender insists on going for repossession rather than allowing you time to sell. There are legal paths you can take on this but the outcome cannot be guaranteed. If you are on benefits while trying to sell, you should inform the Benefits Agency.

When calculating everything, be sure to add up all the costs involved in selling your home (and possibly buying a new one). These can come to alarmingly high figures. I look at buying costs on page 207 and at selling costs on page 138.

Finding an estate agent

It's a bit of a gamble deciding on an estate agent to sell your home. The best way is to ask friends or relatives who they'd recommend. You'll also get some clues as you go around your neighbourhood looking at how various agents present themselves: for example their shop windows and For Sale boards. Although many thousands of agents have gone out of business since the crunch started, the high street still has more than enough to choose from!

The next task is to ask three or four agents to come and value your home. See how this valuation stacks up against the one you've had done for yourself, perhaps by a surveyor. The way an agent behaves will tell you a lot about how they'll deal with your buyers. I know you'll be keen to hear what they'll say on price but this might not be the most important thing when they visit. A good agent will be:

- Punctual
- Smart and well turned out
- Professional in his approach
- Able to listen
- Willing to give you information and tips about how you could improve your chances of selling
- Happy to tell you about their successes with houses similar to yours
- Pleased to show you brochures or websites that display how they'd market your home
- Realistic about the current market
- More interested in getting the best price for you rather than simply making another sale
- Backed up by good office staff able to deal well with people who call about your home

Most estate agents will value your home without charge. Get the opinions of three, bearing in mind that what you'll be looking for is a sale, not empty promises. When you've received all the valuations, use your intuition and common sense to gauge who'll be best. Talk to friends and neighbours locally who may have used your chosen firm before. Ask each agent how many similar properties they've sold in the last month or two. What did they get for them? Discuss how they'd market your home and what they might bring to the party that others cannot.

In a normal market it's the seller who controls this hiring process but, in difficult times, estate agents may have so many properties in stock, with very few buyers looking for them, that they could be very tough about taking your property on, even if you accept their valuation. The central and critical thing will be price. Assuming there's nothing wrong with your place, the agent will want to know that when things are difficult for him and he's laying off staff and shutting offices, he won't be adding yet another unrealistically-priced property to his bank of unsold stock.

Even very good agents tell me they are looking for intense realism over prices and some insist on certain other things such as permission to display a For Sale board, before even considering taking on a property. Many of my contacts say they've stopped listing new properties until they can sell what they already have. Most agents I know have not seen such bad selling conditions for thirty years.

Once you decide on an agent and he has agreed to take on your property, check:

- How he will advertise and otherwise market it
- How and what he will charge for his services

- Whether he will charge for things on top of his normal percentage of the selling price (his commission). If so, what are these extras?
- How you will handle viewings between you
- What staff, other than himself, will be involved
- What he will want you to contribute to the selling process
- The terms of his contract with you
- Whether you intend to use other agents in addition to him
- How long you intend to be bound by a contract with him
- What happens if you find a buyer yourself. Most agents will want you to pay advertising and marketing costs, at least (see below)

When you appoint an estate agent, you are both bound by the contract you sign. Look through this very carefully and seek advice if you're not happy. In a normal market you might give the agent a sole agency for a 'lock-in' period of some months. I've sold properties in buoyant markets where I gave an agent only two weeks to perform before I took the property elsewhere. But things are very different today and it might be that, however good your agent, the shortage of buyers could mean he'll want many months to be able to get a result.

There are several types of contract you can draw up with an estate agent. The main differences, apart from the obvious ones I list, are in how much money you'll agree to pay him.

Sole agency
Here you give the exclusive right to an agent to sell your home. This lasts for a length of time you agree on. At the end of this period, if your property remains unsold, your

contract with him terminates. If you sell the place yourself you pay him nothing except certain expenses that have been agreed on in advance. You cannot claim that you sold the place yourself if the buyer has at any time been in touch with the agent.

Sole selling rights

Under this arrangement you pay the agent his commission whoever sells the property, as he has exclusive rights to sell your home. If you find a buyer yourself, you'll still have to pay him. Ideally, try to avoid this route.

Joint sole agency

Here, two agents act for you at the same time and share the total commission. Your local agent may, for example, have an agreement with a national group. The commission is higher here as two agents have to share it but you increase your marketing reach. Again, if you sell your place yourself, you pay the agents nothing except expenses agreed in advance, provided neither of the agents can claim that they 'introduced' the buyer to the property.

Multiple agency

As the term suggests, you instruct two or more competing agents to market the property at the same time. The agent who gets the sale wins the commission but this is usually set somewhat higher as several agents will be expending time, energy and money trying to sell a house on which they may never see a profit. This type of agency increases your chances of finding a buyer but there can easily be confusion, with one agent offering it to one of their clients after you've already accepted an offer from the client of another agency. To be fair, in a dull market, this is not too big a problem. Some multiple-agency agents don't put that much effort into the job as, they argue, they'll get a smaller return on their efforts compared with handling a house on a sole agency basis. Once again, you'll pay nothing if you sell the property yourself.

Commissions

Commissions can be a tricky subject. Everyone complains that estate agents make too much money. Commissions vary from about one per cent to more than three per cent, according to the nature of the agency, the terms of your contract, and the property being sold. In a bad market, agents are sometimes more than happy to do deals because they are pleased to be able to sell anything. This said, some sellers are so desperate that they are prepared to pay more than usual.

Agents still need to cover their fixed overheads and make a profit, though, so you won't be able to be too picky about doing the best deal. If the fee the agent suggests seems very low, ask them how they can do the same job for less money than others. They may do less advertising, have fewer staff, work out of secondary-location offices, and so on. You'll then have to take a view on all this and decide what you'll lose by going with them.

When appointing an agent, try to get the lowest fee and the shortest lock-in period (so you can quickly change to another agent if things aren't going well). At the moment you should be able to get a good agent to act for you for a one percent commission on the sale price. In this troubled market, though, you need to make sure that the agent is doing his best to ensure that your property stands out from the crowd. Don't be afraid to 'mystery shop' to check that you're getting the service you expected. Your agent should be trying his very best to make that sale.

Property shops charge much less than proper agents but they can do this only by charging a fee at the time you instruct them and keeping it whether or not they get you a sale. Clearly, they have no financial incentive to sell your home. On balance, an estate agent will give you more for your money.

Marketing your property

There's little point having the best property in town if no one knows about it. A good agent will be able to use one or more of many different marketing techniques to find you that buyer. These include:

The agent's website

Now an almost universal tool of the house-hunter. Try out a firm's site before going to a contract with them. Some sites are easy to use and others a real pain. Avoid any firm with a website you personally wouldn't want to use as a buyer. Do a dummy run, pretending to be a buyer for one of their other properties. See how you get treated by the agency's staff when you call up. If they already know who you are, get a friend to do this homework for you. See how quickly the agent sends you details of a properties on their books by e-mail or even by text.

Local advertising

Look in the local papers, local property papers, and other media to see which firm does the best for their clients.

A For Sale board

If your home is on a street, and especially one with considerable traffic, this can be a very effective marketing tool indeed. Many people trawl the area where they think they'd like to buy, just looking at the boards. From a buyer's point of view this can save lots of time because they can see the immediate neighbours at once and get a 'feel' for the property – and, perhaps more import, its surroundings. The agent's well-taken photo in the particulars can never do justice to the delightlful infant school next door that is just out of his well-framed shot!

Look in agents' windows

See how well they present their properties – especially those similar to yours.

Your agent's bank of potential buyers

In normal markets estate agents keep substantial lists of people who are searching for various different types of property. A good agent will, in a normal market, go straight to this bank of potential buyers and get them round to view very quickly – perhaps even before sales particulars have been drawn up. I have bought properties like this several times. Even in a poor market such connections and networking still have their place. This will be especially true if your home is unusual in some way, could be converted to another use, might interest a small builder or developer locally, or could fit in to the investment portfolio of a client of his. In bad times this sort of inside knowledge can make all the difference between a sale and a very long wait. An agent who has been in the area for many years clearly has an advantage here over a newcomer.

Your own contacts

As soon as your home is on the market, get talking to friends, people at work, family and anyone you come across who might be interested. Get used to letting the subject drop in normal conversation. You never know who could have a contact that's just right for your place.

Local or national PR

If your home (or you, to be honest) could be of any interest to the public at large, get your agent to have a piece published about it in your local newspaper. Larger and more unusual properties might make the property pages of the nationals, or the specialist property press. Your agent will advise you. He'll be pleased to listen to your ideas too.

The particulars

The next step is to get some really good pictures taken and to draw up a description of your home, known as 'the particulars'. Your agent will draft the particulars and will usually take some photographs or, if the place is worth it, have a professional photographer do so. The fees of such a pro will be agreed with you in advance. Pictures of this quality are rarely necessary unless you are going to advertise nationally or in specialist property magazines.

The particulars are your shop window and need to be accurate, yet enticing. Details usually included are:

- A description of the house in general ('A substantial, Edwardian house set in half an acre')
- How it stands in the locality ('Half a mile from XYZ mainline station; two good primary schools close by)
- The numbers of rooms and their functions
- The location ('Set in a quiet country lane')
- Its main architectural features/feel ('Completely re-modelled in a contemporary style two years ago')
- Details of parking/garaging
- Details of technical matters that could be of interest ('New central heating last year, completed re-wired five years ago')
- Its energy rating
- Details of energy-saving features ('Solar panels, under-floor heating, double glazing, and a completely insulated loft')
- Special features of interest ('Lovely period features, including original fireplaces and plasterwork')
- Unique features ('Garage converted to a professional-standard woodworking shop')

In other words, anything and everything that you love about your home should be expressed in these particulars. All the details must be scrupulously accurate and you should check that the agent has the details correct. He too will want to be certain that he gets them right as he'll be liable for prosecution if he does not. Once the agent has produced the particulars, go through them carefully and get a friend who knows the place to do so too. I have often helped friends pick up all kinds of slips that do their houses less than justice. Such an outsider could advise you, for example, when to remove something that sounds good to you (because you know the reality) but which doesn't come across that well in writing. Bear in mind that in a poor market your particulars will be screened by potential buyers in a very cursory way, as they'll have so much choice. Try to highlight at least one or two features that will make them remember your details above those of other properties they're considering. They'll be on the look-out for things that put them off. Your particulars mustn't contain anything that could possible do so!

Home Information Packs (HIPs)

The idea behind these packs was to enable everyone involved in buying and selling to get on with the matter quickly and efficiently as some of the key paperwork would already have been done before a buyer viewed a property. From a seller's point of view, it is said that the packs give some confidence that surprises won't suddenly rear their head and delay or, even lose, a sale. Since, and indeed even before, the implementation of HIPs, there has been a lot of controversy over them. Vendors see them as yet another cost to be borne when selling and it has been claimed that they have slowed the housing market, if only a little. Also, some buyers aren't that sure they can trust things they haven't had their own professionals validate for them.

A HIP is simply a pack of information that has to be supplied with every home that goes on the market unless:

- You are selling direct to your family
- The property is not residential
- It is holiday home
- It's being sold under a right-to-buy scheme
- It doesn't have vacant possession
- It is due for demolition

Your agent will give you all the information you need about what your pack should contain but, in general, it should have certain compulsory items:

- An index
- A sale statement, and whether the place is freehold or leasehold

- The results of local authority searches
- Title details
- A current Energy Performance Certificate.

Some documents in the pack are optional. These include:

- A home condition report
- A legal summary
- A home use/contents form
- Additional information for leasehold and commonhold sales, if needed

The trouble is that buyers don't seem interested at the moment in the contents of HIPs, and sellers don't want to spend time or money producing them – especially when experiencing difficulty selling. HIPs will, without doubt, remain an unsatisfactory issue for some time.

For more information on Home Information Packs, go to www.homeinformationpacks.gov.uk

Showing your home

It'll be up to you whether you or a family member shows your place, or whether your agent does. There are pros and cons for each approach.

I think the agent showing is best, on average. It has the advantage of being less personal, and people can feel free to criticise as they go round. This can help the agent get a feel for the market and report back to you what could be done to help your sale along. On one of my sales this worked in my favour, as the agent took me to one side and told me that people might find the smell of our dog off-putting! We took the dog away for future viewings and left all the doors open for an hour or so and no one complained. A sale soon followed.

Of course you may work long hours or be away and so be unable to conduct viewings yourself. Ask your agent in advance whether he'll charge for doing viewings.

Showing people round yourself can be fine provided you don't get personal and certainly never get defensive when people make any sort of adverse comment. I look on page 182 at all the nitty-gritty tips for preparing and showing your home.

Report back at once to the agent if you've shown someone over. Rest assured you'll find it impossible to assess whether or not they'll buy. Don't even bother trying to guess. Over my years of selling properties I cannot, even today, get this right. Some people who seem totally disinterested and un-interested go on to make a good offer and the highly-enthusiastic couple who've put all their furniture in place and allocated the kids' bedrooms, do nothing at all! It's all about personality and given that you won't know the people, it'll be near-impossible for you to judge anything. A really skilled agent can read the body language and hidden agendas well, and this can be a good reason for them doing the viewings. Agents can also ask tricky financial questions of the potential buyers which, frankly, you cannot do.

Accepting an offer

If you are using an agent, the buyer will usually make their offer through him. If they want to deal direct with you, ask them to talk to the agent. Don't get involved yourself or you could mess up your agent's game plan. Most buyers, especially in bad times, offer quite a lot lower than the asking price. Your agent will tell you at once what he thinks about the offer, and it's worth listening to him. True, he'd rather get a sale than no sale, since he makes nothing if there is no sale, but this said, he'll do his best to take everything into account when advising you. This can be very hard because he may feel your 'bird in the hand' is the best you'll get, especially in a falling market.

But the price alone may not be what makes you accept or refuse an offer. I have often taken lower offers from better-qualified buyers. What you need is a result, so a cash buyer or someone without a chain (see below; they may be renting, for example) could be worth a lot of money when the market is uncertain. Someone may be able to move very quickly, for example, which could be a real help if your financial back is against the wall. You'll have to take a view on all this, according to your individual circumstances and your personality style.

Don't forget that an agent may have an interest in recommending one offer over another, especially if providing a mortgage or selling another home on behalf of the buyer. All such interests should be disclosed to you.

If you feel sufficiently confident you can tell your agent that you won't accept X but you will accept Y. You could then come to an agreement somewhere between the two. In good times you can accept two offers at the same time and take two horses to the finishing post, as it were, provided you tell them both. Such 'contract races' are very rare indeed in today's poor market.

When a buyer makes an offer in England and Wales it doesn't bind them to going ahead with the purchase. They can pull out at any time up to the exchange of contracts. When something is sold 'subject to contract' it means that there's still room for talking. This talking most frequently occurs when your buyer's survey shows up nasties that make him re-consider either the entire purchase, or the price. At this stage you can come to an agreement on a lower price or get the work carried out at your expense, after which he will buy. Of course the buyer may use this as an excuse (real or not) to pull out altogether. In a buyer's market he may decide it's all too much aggravation and find another property instead. I'm afraid that in a buyers' market buyers really do have the whip hand. Still, the situation has been exactly the opposite for so many years that perhaps this is a sort of divine justice at last for buyers!

In current circumstances, be sure to keep your home on the market even once you've accepted an offer. Keep showing the place until the day you actually exchange contracts. It's also vital to exchange contracts as fast as possible. Get your solicitor jumping around because buyers can be fickle and, knowing they have the upper hand, may discover something better and leave you in the lurch.

If things go wrong

Selling (or buying) a home is pretty stressful because so many things can go wrong.

Here are a few of the more common ones:

You aren't happy with your estate agent

I mention this because in 2006 more than 8,000 people complained to the ombudsman about estate agents, although obviously only the most serious complaints get this far. If you are unhappy with the way your agent is treating you it's essential to raise the matter with him first.

- Take a partner or a friend with you to discuss the matter. Try to resolve the issue amicably like this
- If this gentle approach doesn't produce the result you want, you could talk to a senior person at the company's head office, should the agency be part of a group
- The next step is to get your local trading standards service involved. You'll find their details in the *Yellow Pages*. A citizen's advice bureau could also be helpful
- If your agent is a member of the National Association of Estate Agents (www.naea.co.uk), or the Ombudsman for Estate Agents' Scheme (www.oea.co.uk) you can approach them for satisfaction. If your estate agent is a surveyor he'll be a member of the Royal Institution of Chartered Surveyors (RICS) and you can contact the Institution via the website at www.rics.org

Your buyer backs out, or reduces their offer

If they back out completely you'll have to start all over again. This will be expensive because you'll have incurred expenses which you'll be unable to get back. Worse still, in some ways, is when a buyer takes you up to the altar rail, as it were, and then announces the marriage is off at the last minute before exchanging contracts. This ploy of 'gazundering' is common and very painful indeed in a poor property market. By the time you've heard the news you could have committed yourself to a new house, organised your life for a move and so on. You could find you have very little choice but to accept a new, lower offer or start the whole process over again in a falling market. This is a very bitter pill to swallow.

Your buyer's surveyor finds problems

This is a not uncommon occurrence. Such adverse survey results have always been used as a basis for renegotiation on price but in a poor market this is even more the case. People don't want, knowingly, to take on somewhere with problems when they are strapped for cash in other ways. When there's a lot of choice they understandably back off and seek out something without problems. Short of reducing the price to help massage the situation back to life, there's little you can do especially when the market is so poor.

The lender's surveyor or valuer finds problems

At the moment, surveyors acting on behalf of lenders are being extra double-cautious. They fear that whatever their valuation of a property, it could be reduced in a short time and, knowing that the buyer will want, say, an 80 or 90% mortgage, may value the place at only this level, whatever the sale price has been agreed. There are a few ways round this. Some lenders are known to use only very conservative valuers. Your estate agent or solicitor will know who they are. Try to convince either of them to get someone else to do the valuation. It can also help if you prepare your house as if it were for a viewing when the surveyor comes round. Clean and tidy might just influence him that little bit. He, like your buyers, will make up his mind very quickly indeed about what your place is worth.

The conditions of sale

In a market where buyers can afford to be picky, you might find that something that never ever bothered you becomes a deal-breaker....or a price-reducer! Then, again, they might suddenly announce they want all the carpets, curtains, the hi-fi, the garden furniture and Uncle Tom Cobbley and all...or the deal's off.

Mortgage problems

Especially today, some of your buyers will have trouble getting a mortgage. I have clients who had been promised a mortgage, only to discover that when it actually came to arranging it on their chosen property, things had changed and the offer was withdrawn. And all this in less than a month! You too might experience the same trouble getting a loan for *your* new home. At the moment borrowing is very difficult indeed, making cash buyers worth their weight in gold. This is one reason for selling if you can, renting and then being a cash buyer yourself.

Planning and Building Regulations (Regs)

If you have made any alterations to your home you must ensure you have all the correct documentation or it could be un-sellable. If you've lost your copies, get more from your local council. Ask your solicitor what to do. In the very worst scenario, even discussing the matter with your local planning department direct could make them come round to inspect and tell you to demolish your illegal work. I always suggest getting an architect, or other professional designer, to look at the work and say whether he could apply for retrospective planning permission on your behalf. This all takes time and money but your home will be left on the shelf unless you sort it out.

Gazundering

I mentioned this horrible, unethical, tactic above. There's little you can do about it but you'll stand a better chance if all negotiations go through the agent. Your emotions are very likely to get in the way and hinder the sale otherwise. Asking for reasons for this change of mind might just embarrass your buyer into saying he has none other than to stuff you!! This is your chance for your agent to justify your price and stick to it, if he can. This said, it's emotional blackmail and gazunderers with cash in their hands usually win in a poor market.

Chains

A chain is a situation that occurs when a queue of buyers and sellers are all inter-linked simultaneously, trying to sell and buy their homes. Each transaction is only as strong as the weakest link around it. This means that if you have a chain of, say, five properties, you have to have only one party that can't get a mortgage and the whole system falls apart. No one moves home!

This failure of a chain causes about one in three house-buying transactions to fall through. The house-buying system is intrinsically flawed because under English law anyone can back out of a proposed transaction right up to the moment of the exchange of contracts. In Scotland, where a contract occurs the moment a sale is agreed, such aggravation is much less common.

Needless to say, the costs in terms of energy, nerves and money are very high if someone does back out. All your legal fees, any survey costs, and much more can be lost in a moment. You have no redress from any of the other parties. And they may just have changed their minds...not come across some fatal flaw in their buying or selling plans. Even when contracts have been exchanged – after which, technically the buyer forfeits the ten per cent deposit he has paid if he decides not to proceed – this still may not give you the confidence you'd like. People not infrequently back out of a contract at this stage. It has happened to me twice in recent years. Whether or not you feel justified in retaining their deposit will be up to you. I didn't do so, and I'm glad I did not.

It's because chains are so stressful that it's best, if possible, to put yourself in a position where you are in cash at the time of buying. This gives the person you are buying from a lot of confidence that at least *you* won't let them down. Of course someone in the chain could still let *you* down! In a bad market, if you can possibly find yourself with cash in your pocket when buying it'll make life considerably easier. It will also mean you can do a better deal on the price.

Avoiding chains is, of course, the ideal. But this is easier said than done. You can do your best to satisfy yourself on the status of those around you but this is very difficult in practice. For your part, ensure that everything is absolutely right with your place so you don't find yourself as the weakest link, and that you have your mortgage in place before you even start looking for somewhere to buy. A way out of a broken chain is to obtain bridging finance from a bank but this is expensive and hard to come by in a poor housing market. It is to be avoided at all costs.

If your property isn't selling

Until about late 2007, I'd have given you a whole range of things to do that could get your estate agent cracking and getting the best price for you. However, things are now dramatically different and even very good agents are struggling to make sales.

This said, there are things that are worth considering before giving up. Arrange a meeting with your agent to discuss:

Feedback from the viewings you've had

There are always lessons to be learned. Some things you won't be able to change, no matter what viewers have said. But there could be ways of making your place more attractive. Consider the adverse comments when you hear them from your agent and between you decide what could be done.

Phone-calling

Ask him whether his people have been chasing potential buyers, and following up viewings as they should. It's helpful to discover why people who said they didn't want to view, made their decision. What could you do to alter the particulars to get round this? Did a photo give a bad impression? Was there something misleading that disappointed? See what drive-by viewers thought. What put them off? Buyers usually report something to the agent (and a good agent always asks), even if they just drove by. What could you do to address their criticisms?

Spreading the word

Has your agent actually passed your details on to other branches in the area? I've been shocked to find this hadn't occurred on several of my sales. I know that over-stocked branches might not want more houses to sell but you need to convince your agent that someone in that area might just be your buyer.

Marketing

Get your agent to show you the ads and PR he has done. What could you do to help? Would you be prepared to pay for a special, perhaps colour, advert in a newspaper or specialist property magazine? Would a special mailing to a sub-group of his clients help? Suggest you help towards the costs of any of your ideas, or even pay for them all.

Price

This is where the going gets tough. Talk honestly about whether or not a price reduction would help get the result you both want. Look at other comparable properties he has just sold. How does yours compare? It's perfectly reasonable to make such comparisons, because your buyers certainly will! If you are buying somewhere after selling yours, it could be that you can take less for your place and negotiate with your seller to reduce his price by the same amount. This could carry on right down the chain. Anything's worth a try in this market.

Selling your home yourself

Selling your home yourself isn't that difficult in normal markets. I have done so several times and it went very well. Whether or not it's the way to go for you, now, tempting as it is to save paying an estate agent, is another question.

You really have to ask yourself:

- Am I any good at selling *anything*?
- Can I set aside my personal feelings and emotions about my home enough to see it as an object to be sold?
- Can I arrive at a sensible, realistic selling price that will attract buyers?
- Am I prepared to put in the time and effort needed to market the property?
- Will I be able to negotiate with a buyer in a tough, buyers' market where he'll have masses of choice?
- Have I got the stamina to cope with tiny numbers of viewers who, when they do show up, will be picky and looking for a reason not to buy?
- Have I got that one hundred per cent commitment to selling I'll need in this market? If you are half-hearted, you'll never sell. An agent is never half-hearted, it's his business to sell
- Do my personal life circumstances allow me to give this job the time and energy it deserves? If you are ill, experiencing relationship or financial difficulties, have business problems, or are suffering in any other way in life, trying to sell your own place in this market could just be a step too far. Think about it very carefully before taking it on

Advantages of selling it yourself:

- It'll save you money
- You know your home and the area better than anyone else
- You can answer any questions as they occur (see page 201)
- You'll be in control of the whole process
- You can choose where you want to advertise and can even approach the local paper's property writer to get some PR
- You can decide which photos show off your place to its best
- You can list your home on a specialist website as well as anybody
- You could print a flyer and distribute it to a few hundred local homes. How about local notice boards in shop windows? Put ads in all the local publications you can think of, from church newsletters to school and other publications.
- You can design and make your own For Sale board. It could look so unfamiliar to local passers-by that they take notice of if more than they would of a local agent's professionally-made board
- You can employ friends and family to act as your 'agents'. Offer them a reward (commission) if they find a buyer. Just talking about your place at work, pub or gym, could land you your result
- You can organise viewings to suit only yourself and the viewers
- You can enter into a personal relationship with your intended buyer which can help the game along
- You will find that some buyers dislike agents and would rather deal direct with you

Disadvantages of selling it yourself:

- You may not have the sales skills, especially in a hard market
- You may find it too stressful if other things in life are tough
- You certainly won't have a network of potential buyers at your fingertips
- You'll be at the mercy of the market and could put yourself in a weak position
- Unless you are a skilled negotiator in other areas of life you could find you're out of your depth when financial issues get tough
- An agent will have tried-and-tested ways of showing off properties in their particulars, press ads, and on their websites and will carry out basic checks on applicants, all of which saves time and money if a sale goes ahead. Do you really want to learn how to do all this?
- You might want to consider the security aspects of showing complete strangers around your home on your own. Many people are not happy to do so
- Solicitors and other agents might not be comfortable discussing details of other people in a chain in which you are involved. This lack of information could have a serious effect on making a sale, especially in bad times

In the final analysis you'll have to decide on the balance of these pros and cons according to your personal situation and skills base. You could even combine the two methods. I have, on several occasions, appointed an agent and also told them I'd try to sell myself. Just be certain that your contract with the agent allows you to do this without paying him the whole commission should you come up trumps. It's only fair that he receives something for his efforts but this will need to be clarified before you and he start to market your home.

Costs of selling your home

Although the costs involved in *selling* your home are usually less than when *buying*, they're still very real, numerous and unwelcome, and soon add up.

Getting ready

How much time, money and effort you put into preparing your home for sale will, of course, be up to you. I look at some of these issues on page 182. But here just let's think about repairs, cleaning, making good etc that will make your place desirable and stand out from the rest. Take advice from your surveyor or estate agent on what they think is worth spending money on at this stage of the game. OK, the place would sell better with a conservatory but you just might not have the cash for such a major set-piece....and it might not make its cost back. Talk through what can be achieved for your budget.

Home Information Pack (HIP)

This (see page 122) will cost money, and you as seller will have to pay for it. This usually comes to only a few hundred pounds but even this can seem a lot if your financial back is against the wall.

Estate agent's fees

You'll know well in advance what these will be but they still need paying. This will be your largest single cost when selling, so it's worth doing the best deal you can.

Solicitor's fees

As with your agent, you'll be able to know up-front what these costs will be. Sometimes an unforeseen problem crops up which requires a lot more legal time to sort out. Even if this were to occur, no solicitor will just let a huge bill mount up behind your back. Many solicitors make a substantial proportion of their income by doing conveyancing work. In these difficult days you'll be able to do a good deal on fees.

Removal costs

A ray of light here is that many companies are keen for work so you'll get a very competitive price.

> As a rough guide, if you are selling a property worth £200,000 your costs will be about £6,000 (not allowing anything for what you do to the house to make it more sellable).

Sale and lease-back and sale and rent-back schemes

Some companies help borrowers who are in financial difficulties by buying their home *from them* and renting it back *to them*. Such deals are sometimes called 'flash sales' because the whole transaction can be accomplished so fast. It usually takes less than a month. They are more often known as sale and lease-back or sale and rent-back schemes. They aren't the same as equity release schemes which allow people who have paid off their mortgage to sell their home and retain the right to live in it. I look at these on page 170.

The problem with sale and lease-back (and similar) schemes is that you no longer own your home and you have no protection under FSA regulations. This means you could be evicted if you fail to make your rental payments. And such companies rarely pay the going rate for your home when they buy it in the first place. Clearly these solutions to a personal financial crisis have serious drawbacks. Take advice from an IFA, solicitor, or Citizen's Advice Bureau before entering into any such agreement.

Selling your home at auction

More than 65,000 properties are sold at over one thousand auctions each year in the UK but it remains a minority way of selling domestic properties compared with going through an estate agent. The main reasons people choose to sell their home at auction are: if they have a really special or unusual property that needs to find its price level in the open market, or if they need a quick sale.

The advantages of selling at auction are many. First, you know on the day of the auction that you have sold and for how much. This can be vital and indeed a life-saver if you're selling in a financial crisis. A second benefit can be that from the day you instruct an auctioneer, things can be made to happen very quickly as auction houses usually have a very short marketing phase. Third, there's no opportunity for 'gazundering' or other game-playing by the buyer and, if your property is priced right (the auctioneer will be a good guide on this), you'll be very likely to get a sale on the day. In normal markets, around eighty percent of all properties taken to auction sell…and this can rise further if a buyer deals with the auctioneer after the sale day. Today, a smaller percentage sells as even carefully-considered reserve prices are not reached. As this book went to press, I was at an auction at a London saleroom where only about 40% of all the property found a buyer.

But a major advantage is that there is no chain. This is a real winner when the market is rough.

There are more than eighty auctioneers to choose from throughout the country. Research auctioneers' catalogues and advertisements to see which auction house in your area suits you and your property best. Choose one that deals with your type of property on a daily basis. Try to find the auction house that'll do the best marketing for your sort of house. Unless they get the potential buyers through their front door on sale day, you won't get the best price. Go to a local house auction to see how they do things and to judge for yourself how appropriate they'd be for you.

When choosing the people to deal with, try to assess how efficient and pleasant they are. Ask them about national marketing if you think your place needs or deserves it. As with estate agents, it's unwise to go with the firm that values your home at the highest price. Take an overall view. After all, it'll be the bidders on the day who'll value it, and for that you'll have to rely on the auction house getting the right people there.

How do you pay?

Auctioneers charge an entry fee to have your property listed with them. These fees vary according to how good the catalogue is, and how extensive the marketing is. The big auction houses charge up to £2,500 per lot. Sale fees are on top of this and are usually between one and a half and three per cent, with a minimum fee of anything up to two or three thousand pounds. Don't be overly-influenced by a low entry fee (or a low commission on the sale). What you need is a result, and this could mean paying a bit more.

If you withdraw your property before the sale day, your auctioneer will reduce your fee. If you sell on the day and the buyer backs out you'll still have to pay but, here again, the fee will be reduced. If you enter into a sole agency agreement with the auction house they'll be entitled to their full fee if you sell the house through someone other than them in the period of time you've agreed.

What you have to do

When offering your home to be sold at auction, you have to provide evidence that you are who you say you are and that the place is yours to sell. You must also give an absolute undertaking that the auctioneer has the right to sell for you. In other words, you can't go back on your agreement with them on the sale day. You will also be unable to bid for your home yourself on the day once you have instructed your auctioneer to bid on your behalf. This makes sense because once you set your reserve price, you are, in effect, saying 'I won't sell for less than this' and the auctioneer then bids up to just below that level on your behalf to ensure that it doesn't go for less. The essence of this is that, in law, an auction sale is rendered illegal if two people bid for the same property by arrangement. Other things you'll need to do are to provide exact and accurate details of your home for the catalogue, and to discuss a guide price and then agree the reserve price in writing several days before the sale.

As with any house sale, you'll need to instruct a solicitor and most auction houses will ask for an indemnity to the effect that details supplied by you and your solicitor are accurate. This is all the more important than when selling through an estate agent because auctioneers have to be as certain as they can that the facts about the property are correct, because the deal is clinched the moment the gavel comes down. They are also careful because they are bound by the Property Misdescriptions Act of 1991. Get your solicitor working at the same time as instructing the auction house and make sure he understands how urgently you need things done.

A major job for you is to work with the auctioneer to come to an agreed guide price and subsequently a reserve price for your home. He'll have a pretty good idea of what sort of price to put in the catalogue as a guide. You'll want this to be low-ish to attract buyers but not so low as to create frustrated purchasers on the day. A day or two before the sale you should discuss the final reserve price with the auctioneer. The guide price and the reserve price (the price below which you will not sell), are usually fairly close.

Quite frequently the auctioneer will receive an offer before the sale day. He'll tell you at once and advise you, knowing his market, what he thinks is best to do. Although the auctioneer will be aware of anyone who has shown an interest in your place, it can be near-impossible to know how to advise you as there could be just that one fantastic buyer who'll turn up on the day, of whom the auctioneer is unaware. Some, even very professional, auction buyers find themselves disappointed on a lot they'd intended to get and suddenly decide, on the spur of the moment, to buy something else they fancy, sight unseen.

When fixing your reserve be guided by the auctioneer, as selling in this way isn't like using other methods. Setting the reserve too high could easily result in no sale at all. This puts you in a bad position after the sale when buyers will try to get a bargain knowing that you are on the back foot and there's now no competition for them as there was in the auction room. This is a bad position to be in, especially in a poor market.

The fixed reserve price is also vital on the day of the auction before bidding begins, as the auctioneer is allowed by law to bid on your behalf (provided you are not bidding too) until he reaches one incremental bid below the reserve. A good auctioneer can read the room and get enthusiasm going, persuading people to bid that little bit more than they had intended. Once your reserve is set the auctioneer will sell at that figure (or, preferably, above it if there are bidders) without referring to you. This is the reality of auction selling....there are no second thoughts! Don't for a moment imagine that if your place fails to sell in the room, the highest bidder will be chasing you afterwards to get the property at that price. He won't! He'll know you're at a disadvantage and will home in for the kill.

If your solicitor comes to the sale (and even if he doesn't) there will be an exchange of contracts there and then and the buyer will deposit ten per cent of the sale price with the auction house, or your solicitor. Either way, your money is perfectly safe. This said, you can't get your hands on it at this stage. Your solicitor will now talk to your buyer's legal representative and they'll take things forward to completion of the deal within twenty working days. Your buyer must comply with this or he'll lose not only the property but also possibly, a lot more money. Unfortunately, in these difficult times, some people who have been promised a mortgage, put their deposit down and find that they cannot honour the contract because their mortgage offer is withdrawn in the twenty working day period. This can be a nightmare.

If your home doesn't sell on the day, or immediately after the sale, you could talk to the auctioneer about putting it in again at a lower price. Or you could consider using another auction house.

Chapter 6
ALTERNATIVES TO
SELLING UP

When times are hard it can appear that the only way forward is to sell up and get out. But this may be avoidable unless your back is against the wall. For example, when builders are in financial trouble, which they are during property downturns, it can be a great time to build. A mid-2008 study by a leading UK high street bank reported a 20% jump in the numbers of people asking for money to improve their homes. Of these, half said they were doing improvements to increase their chances of selling. A survey of 500 estate agents in June 2008 found that about half of all their vendors had withdrawn their properties from the market to spend money on improvements.

Just how wise it is to put more money into your home like this will depend very much on the individual home and your local property climate. If you are making the improvements so you can stay and have a better home, rather than subjecting yourselves to the poor market, then this is fine. But spending large amounts of cash in order to sell may not be effective. Of all the things that are possible, only spending money on decorating and tarting up the property cosmetically will definitely pay for themselves in the short term.

It's a good idea to get a couple of estate agents round to give you an opinion on what's worth doing, before you even start on anything. They'll be aware of what current buyers really care about in this market. At this stage it's probably sensible only to tackle deal-breaking issues.

When thinking about financing such changes, be careful how you borrow. Don't go for a 'secured loan' as this is lent against the value of your property and would effectively become a second charge on your home at a time when you won't want to be increasing your risk, should the value of your place fall. People used to ask their lender for a 'further advance' – in effect increasing their mortgage – but even if you can get a lender to agree to this it might be dangerous if it shrinks your available equity.

There are many possible alternatives to selling up and this chapter looks at the main ones. You can:

- Extend
- Renovate or re-model
- Divide your home
- Sell off a garden plot
- Take in another generation
- Release Equity
- Make money from your property
- Make extra money in other ways

Extend

For every new-build in the UK there are probably four serious-sized extensions being done at any one time. There are many good reasons for extending your home rather than moving. It's usually far less disturbing for the family; it's often a good way of enhancing the existing equity in your home; and it can be just the right answer when the housing market is unstable or falling and your property is hard to sell. You can be sure that the housing cycle will regain its stability one day and that eventually you'll have a more valuable property as a result of your hard work. Look at what neighbours have done, to see what you're likely to be allowed. If you want to do something that bucks this trend, be prepared to spend time, energy and money. Think very hard about doing this in a bad market. You may feel you can outsmart the market by tarting up your place to an above-average specification but, believe me, this can also be the way to disaster. All you need to do is to create something that's 'good enough'.

There's no doubt that building an extension causes disruption and stress because you'll, in effect, be living on a building site. But, overall, this can still involve substantially less aggravation than moving – and could, given the high fixed costs of moving home (see pages 138 and 207), actually save money. Keep reminding yourself why you're building rather than moving and you'll keep focused on the essentials.

There are several basic options:
- Convert existing space (such as a loft or garage) into living accommodation

- Build over an existing structure (for example, a granny flat over the garage)
- Extend your existing structure's footprint
- Go down into your basement, or create a new one

You can also build a completely new structure of some kind in your garden.

Before you decide to extend your home, it's worth considering a few things. These could all be important at the best of times but in a falling market they can make all the difference between success and failure.

Ceiling price

Whilst it's tempting to imagine that spending, say, £25,000 will add a similar value to your home, this may not be the case. In most streets and neighbourhoods, there's a ceiling price for any given type of house. It's possible to exceed this on occasion and still come out on top but it's far easier to over-spend and then lose out if you're not going to stay for a long time. Truth be told, it can be hard to know how long you'll stay when the economy isn't great and you might lose your job. It's also a fact that ceiling prices change a lot when there's a property downturn. Be sure to listen to what estate agents or surveyors are saying when planning your revised ceiling price. Whilst on this subject, don't be seduced by *asking prices*....what you need to know is what places like yours are actually selling for. Spending a bit on a surveyor with good local knowledge can help you learn exactly what buyers will pay for at the moment, what types of properties are in short supply, and so on.

I know it's very un-glamorous and never the subject of TV programmes but it could be that the best way you can spend your £25,000 is by replacing your roof, re-wiring, painting and decorating, and making other necessary changes. This could, paradoxically, add more value to your home than an extension. Although most of us tend to think 'sexy update' when we talk about an extension, provably the best way of spending cash is, in this order:

- Ensuring the existing building is safe, structurally up to date and well-maintained
- Adding living space
- Adding 'lifestyle'

In 2006, a Halifax survey found that the features people most wanted to add were not the items valuers ruled most advantageous to property value. People most favoured a new kitchen but valuers were emphatic that adding floor area was more effective. To be fair, replacing a kitchen came second on their list. Other things they said added value were painting and decorating, extensions, extra rooms, and a new bathroom. Garages are no longer much wanted (for cars, anyway) and don't add a lot of value, but off-street parking certainly does. The value of some properties rises by ten per cent after adding parking. This said, you won't much care about adding parking if your need is for more accommodation rather than moving. In fact, any extension you add will need to be viewed in the long term as you may be doing it so you can stay living where you are.

People intending to make changes for their own use say they want to add: gadgets (such as flat-screen TVs); Jacuzzis, hot tubs or saunas, a pool, or even a gym. But very few of these add value to your home when it comes to selling. Anything that creates extra maintenance can be an actual turn-off. The best example of this is a pool. Huge numbers of people are put off homes with a pool, the main reason being the effort and money it costs to look after it. As with all personalised home improvements, only ever consider them if you are certain you'll live there long enough to enjoy them personally. How long this might be is hard to say but somewhere between five and ten years makes sense. If in doubt, only do things that answer your immediate needs, as opposed to your wants. Never lose sight of why you're doing the extension....to provide you with living space more cheaply than moving.

Room balance

I've looked at ceiling price and warned against over-extending. A word now about room balance. If you're contemplating an extension, be sure that the overall balance of accommodation is about right. Loads of bedrooms, with few reception rooms (or vice versa) confuses buyers, should you need to sell in a hurry. Also balance what you'd like to live with versus what buyers actually want. Get an estate agent in before you go ahead with an extension of any size. They'll know what adds value in your area, or even in your exact type of house.

Closely allied to this balance is being careful not to ruin the architectural style of your property. Try to retain or enhance original features, refurbishing them, or replacing them like for like when it's impossible to save them. Very clever designers can create additions that are strikingly different from the existing but the outcome can be hard to predict. The best of the old alongside the best of the new can work very well but both need to be cleverly detailed.

When planning your extension or renovation be careful to get the flow of the living space right. Consider talking this all through with a good designer. Even if you don't intend to use one for your project, layout could be one area worth spending an hour on with a paid expert. Listen, too, to agents about this as they'll know what other people have done in your area and what has worked in homes like yours.

What else instead?
Rather than crashing on with the expense, stress and disruption of an extension, have you carefully considered what else you could do instead? Some possibilities include:

- Using stores or spare rooms for accommodation (dumping, giving away, or long-term storing the contents of the rooms)
- Thinking about the under-stairs area for a small home office
- Getting rid of your dining room and transforming it into more useable space
- Converting the end of a garage
- Building something in the garden

Above all, it's vital to discover what's happening in your local market so you don't do anything that could prejudice the value of your home, should you need to sell sooner than you intended.

Rules and regulations
Just because you already own a property doesn't mean you can do what you like to it. You'll still need to think about planning, building regulations, and possibly listed building consent, if this applies. You'll also need to get formal permission from your landlord if your home is leasehold, as opposed to freehold. It's wise to make this enquiry your first task as your landlord may quash the whole idea.

Once you've decided what you want, it's a good idea to talk things through with your local planners. This said, I favour professional advice as a short-cut whenever possible. An hour with a good local surveyor, designer or builder could save all kinds of heartache with the planners because you'll quickly know what permission is needed, probably after a brief visit to your home. You can then bat ideas back and forth without tainting your relationship with the planning department. They, after all, are not in business to give you free design advice. Only someone acting in your best interests can do this. Small extensions may not need to involve a designer at all as they can be professionally handled from start to finish by a competent contractor. Choosing one who's worked for a neighbour is a great idea as you'll benefit from lessons learned on their project.

Building regulations apply pretty much as to a completely new build but can be simplified a little as the new structure will become part of your existing home. For example, when it comes to energy-efficiency regulations you just have to build your new part to the latest regs. Newly-installed windows and boilers have to come up to the latest standards, of course. Part M (disabled access) of the Building Regulations is simpler because all you need do is to ensure that your new work hasn't made it more difficult for a disabled person. Any house constructed after 1999 should already be Part M compliant.

Permitted development rights

'Permitted development rights' enable you to do certain things to your home without obtaining planning permission. In some areas of the country ('designated areas') these rights are very restricted and, if you live in a conservation area, the Norfolk or Suffolk Broads, or a national park, or an Area of Outstanding Natural Beauty you could find things very tricky. In some areas local planners may issue an Article 4 Direction which means you can't do things that in other areas would be permitted development. If you live in a listed building you're into another loop entirely.

What constitutes 'permitted development' differs in each part of the UK and the Republic of Ireland; seek local advice. In October 2008, the rules governing permitted development changed dramatically. Between 1997 and 2007 the numbers of domestic planning applications doubled to 330,000. The new rules will remove approximately 80,000 households a year from the planning system. Local Authorities will be less burdened and more able to focus on larger applications. Hopefully, this will mean that local planning officers will be able to give a better service. The new measures will also save the nation up to £50 million each year.

The 2008 changes will allow some people to build both up and out without obtaining specific planning permission - which previously often cost as much as £1,000 in planning fees. They will also make it easier if you want to improve rather than move at a time like this when the property market is so difficult. And many people are choosing this route in preference to the trials of selling and buying.

Rear extensions and loft conversions
Terraced: loft conversions can be up to 20 centimetres back from the eaves or have a maximum volume of 40 cubic metres. Also, a single- or two-storey rear extension can go back a maximum of 3 metres from the original house.
Semi-detached: as terraced but with a maximum loft volume of 50 cubic metres.
Detached: as for terraced but with a maximum volume of 50 cubic metres. In addition, a rear extension can either be a single storey going 4 metres back from the original house, or a two-storey one going 3 metres back.

Ground floor rear extensions in conservation areas will be permitted (but loft conversions in such areas will continue to be restricted).

Driveways and parking areas
New driveways or parking areas over 5 square metres will not require planning permission if made from surfaces that allow water to soak through. A new user-friendly guide for builders and DIY-ers is available at: www.communities.gov.uk/publications/planningandbuildi ng/pavingfrontgardens

Part of all these changes is a new section of the planning portal website (www.planningportal.gov.uk/uploads /hhg/houseguide.html) This is an interactive guide that helps the public understand planning requirements when making home improvements. You can click on the part of the house you want to change and it explains the rules. Changes to the rules also mean that home-owners can install solar panels without planning permission.

Building regulations still apply to conversions and extensions even if they don't need planning permission under the new permitted development rules.

Welcome though these changes are, it might have been even better to have given local authorities flexibility to set their own permitted development rights because they understand their unique housing and environmental situations best.

You'll need to apply for planning if more than half your land area will be covered by existing buildings and your new extension together. This rule applies to the original house (defined as how it was first built, or as it was on 1 July, 1948 if built before that date). This takes into account extensions that could have been done by others over the years. Most garden development can be carried out only on the basis that it doesn't become living accommodation. This means that to be within permitted development it has to be a home office, or something that couldn't be said to be a house.

You'll need to consult a professional when negotiating your way through the Party Wall Act. This legislation governs what you can do to a wall (or other structure, including a floor or a driveway) you share with a neighbour. It applies to anyone living in a flat; or a semi-detached, or terraced house. Even if you come to an amicable agreement with your neighbour this doesn't mean you won't need to consider planning or building regs. Party wall regulations also apply to any new, free-standing walls up to an existing building or astride a boundary line and any excavations you make that are close to a neighbour's property. This means the Act could affect you even if you live in a detached property.

Adjacent property owners can do one of three things: Consent in writing; Object in writing or; Ignore you. If they do nothing within 14 days a dispute has legally arisen. The best way to settle matters is amicably between you. If you can't achieve this then you'll need to appoint 'An Agreed Surveyor' who'll draw up an 'Award'.

There's a lot of talk about rights to light. In England and Wales a right to light occurs if someone has enjoyed it from a particular opening in their building for more than twenty years. Get professional advice to help you make calculations about how much light would be 'stolen' by your development. These are civil matters between neighbours and have nothing to do with planning. A specialist company,

Right of Light Consulting, can help with this (www.right-of-light.co.uk)

What's possible?

Going up: Loft conversions can provide meaningful extra space that's well suited to that extra bedroom; bathroom; store room; home office; or playroom. You'll need professional advice early on here as your roof structure and other issues may rule it out. If other, similar, homes in your street have one you're probably going to be OK. In general you'll need:

- Enough head height (ideally 500mm above your head or a minimum of 2.3 metres from the underside of the roof ridge to the ceiling in the room below)
- Enough width (about 3 metres or more between purlins – the horizontal beams that hold up the roof)
- A simple roof structure (one with 'hips', for example, encroaches badly on available space)
- Sufficient room to put in a proper staircase from the floor below (with a head height of a minimum of 2 metres)
- No friendly bats in residence (they may be protected and thus have to stay put!)
- No chimneys obstructing your space
- Water tanks that can be easily re-sited (or you'll be paying many hundreds of pounds to replace your system with a pressurised one that needs no loft tanks)
- The correct party wall permissions if you intend to insert steels into your neighbours' walls

Arrangements for escape in the event of fire are also strictly regulated but making such escape possible can involve quite serious alterations to structures on the floors below. On occasion, the provision of a staircase and all the associated fire safety works can mean so many expensive alterations to the existing house that you may decide that a loft conversion isn't worth the trouble. It's a trade-off. If your loft conversion is, in effect, a third floor (which is likely) you'll also have to provide a window large enough to get out of in case of fire. I always make these exits larger than required by law, if only because many of us are overweight.

Current insulation regulations mean you'll have to install at least 120mm of a board such as Kingspan, and this plus the ventilation requirements and ceiling lining will further reduce your head height.

If your roof structure is formed by trusses, there'll be more work and expense involved creating a suitable space in your roof than if you have a 'cut' (traditional) roof structure. It may even not be possible to do it at all.

Going down: Basements are very common in the US and in several Continental countries but rare in the UK. In fact, many highly competent professionals in the UK know nothing much about them. Building a basement as you construct a new property needn't cost the earth but doing so under an existing structure is difficult and expensive. Planners vary in their approach to basement conversions and extensions. Such works definitely require planning permission and can be the subject of heated discussions. In general, storage, hobby rooms, gyms and pools go down relatively well with planners.

Some older houses have basements that can be converted. These homes have suspended timber ground floors, which makes things easier than if there's a concrete ground floor slab. Going into the ground is by far the most costly way of adding space to your home as it involves: digging out and removing soil; ensuring the existing structure is sound and supported (perhaps by underpinning the outside walls of the original house); ensuring it is all dry (involving tanking and other more sophisticated water-proofing methods); supporting your existing ground floor and the loads of the walls on it; and so on. Providing light, ventilation, foul-water drainage, and access can also add challenges. You'll need to create a space in your existing ground floor for a staircase down to your new space and this can often be hard to achieve.

Going into the ground usually costs about double that of adding space any other way.

Going out: This is the way most people extend. A conservatory is a fashionable way of achieving this. It will bring light into your life but can rob it from the rooms off which it opens. There are issues too about heat loss. You are required to have a set of exterior quality doors between your conservatory and the room on to which it is built. If you want to do away with this you'll need to convince the building regs officers that you can and will make up for this loss of heat conservation by improving your glazing standards in other areas of the house to compensate. There's a general rule that the amount of glazing in a house shouldn't be more than twenty five per cent of the floor area but deals can be done by improving glazing quality and other heat conservation measures elsewhere.

For obvious reasons, it's generally more cost effective to build two storeys whenever you can, as the high cost of foundations and roofing are then shared over the two floors. This said: you may not want something this big; it could annoy the neighbours more; it could make planning more difficult to get; and you may not be able to afford it.

Building challenges

Extending your home creates all kinds of problems during the build. Even quite seasoned builders say they'd rather do a new build for themselves than make substantial alterations to their existing home.

Access is always a problem compared with working on a new site. Parking and materials storage can be tricky, and problems with neighbours can be made worse. Scaffolding may have to infringe on your neighbour's land or buildings, and it's often impossible to get meaningful-sized plant round the back, making hand digs more common. Your inability to store large amounts of anything will increase the actual cost of goods. In general, extensions cost about one fifth more than comparable new-builds on a site but this doesn't take into account the aggravation factor, which can be huge. Men around your home; dirt and dust everywhere, even with good screening; their use of your kitchen and toilets; worries about leaving your children in the presence of people you don't know; falling out with the neighbours; and security issues are a just a few of the headaches that go with creating a major extension. The whole thing is also under your nose day and night, perhaps for many months and if you're a 'private' person the sheer presence of so many people all the time can be unpleasant.

This said, some people like having their builders around and are sad when they go. For some extenders this form of building gives them what they want without a move. It's also possible to keep a close eye on progress if you are project managing, and security is less of a headache. Be sure to check with your insurance company before you lift a hammer. Your existing mortgage company will also need to know what you are intending to do, even if you aren't borrowing cash from them to do the work.

Renovate or remodel

This can be an attractive option compared with moving because there's something there already, which can make planning easier. You may find yourself going this route and extending a little too. You will also be aware that your existing house has features that are worth keeping, or indeed that make you want to do the project at all. The building's planning history can have a big effect on what you're allowed to do. Previous refusals are usually a bad start but may not be terminal! See exactly what was refused and why. A better design, or your intelligent and persistent grappling with a problem could make planning possible for you when previous owners failed. If planning has been refused at appeal, or there have been several recent refusals, you'll probably be better off forgetting the project.

Once you've decided on going the renovation route, the first job is to have your place surveyed. You'll need to know exactly what the state of the structure is and what you're likely to be in for, apart from the obvious things you can see for yourself. Unless your home is listed, you can make whatever changes you like inside. If it *is* listed you could be in for a heavy fine or even a jail sentence if you alter even *interior* details without listed building consent. When renovating in towns and cities you'll be expected to use external materials that are the same as, or sympathetic with, existing ones. And you won't be able to do anything that adversely affects the lives of those around you. Development in a village must retain the feeling of the area and not appear out of place in scale or design. Planners usually baulk at anything that increases the size and 'mass' of a building significantly; structures that are out of keeping architecturally; and so on.

The problem is deciding when it's worth using as much of the existing as you can and when it makes sense to take something down and start again. Depending on your plans for the project it is usually best to retain as much of the existing property as possible, especially if there are good architectural features that are specific to the locality. All this can be a very fine call indeed and even highly-experienced and sensitive professionals may disagree.

The minute you decide to demolish something you add considerably to your budget. If you discover asbestos or some other noxious substance, serious timber rot, or other major structural nasties, your costs can quickly escalate. If you're recreating something that looks like, or even has architectural references to what was there before, it's worth keeping everything you possibly can during demolition and designing the old materials and features into your new work. Planners love this and it'll save you money, too.

The problem for many home-owners going the renovation route is that they want something much bigger than already exists. In general, planners don't want to see a cottage replaced by a mansion and talk about the 'impact' of the new house compared with what was there. This sort of situation can often benefit from the wiles and skills of a professional planning consultant. All this is, to some extent, a game and there are ways of playing the game that give you a better chance of winning.

But whatever your plans for renovating, be assured it'll cost a lot more than building from scratch or putting on a simple extension. Preserving the best of the old and building around it is costly and slow; re-creating historical features is painstaking and pricy; and everything takes a lot longer, from planning to construction. This said, I like renovating because it's possible to end up with something characterful and special, compared with even a very good newly-built extension. It depends on how much you really want to go this extra mile, as to whether it'll appeal to you or not.

In general, the more personal effort you put into your renovation, the more long-term value you'll add.

Whatever you're thinking of doing – extending or renovating – talk to the neighbours early as they'll have views on the matter and may be in a position to stop your development.

Divide your home

It can be tempting to sell a part of your house to a family member if you need to release some cash – while at the same time giving them a home. Mixing business with pleasure often back-fires, so it's vital for both parties to take independent legal advice. Each party should also discuss the matter with their own IFA with respect to taxation (including gift taxes and Inheritance Tax).

If your home is too large for you it could be possible to divide it up into units that can be sold off separately. Talk to a surveyor or estate agent about values and very early on take the advice of a designer who could advise you on how the place could be split and the likelihood of the planners allowing you to do it. Legal issues are an early consideration as there could be restrictive covenants that preclude the whole project, whatever anyone advises you. This way of splitting your home is a long shot that's likely to apply to only a few people, but it can work very well. One major advantage is that you can stay put in your own home, if only a part of it.

Sell off a garden plot

If you are lucky enough to have a large garden, it can make sense to get planning on it and sell it on. Incidentally, this tactic can also apply to any major alterations to your home for which you have obtained planning permission. You don't have to build that extension, or whatever: selling on with just the planning in place can greatly add value.

Back to your garden. Legally, everything's simple as you already own the deeds and legal title. Just to be safe, though, talk to your solicitor before you move a muscle. He might just discover a covenant that precludes you from doing what you want. A good solicitor with local knowledge might also know about the likelihood of your getting planning. Given the shortage of land for new homes, planners are keen to use every piece of building land they can within built-up areas. It used to be thought that the term 'brownfield site' meant old factories and derelict sites but in fact it applies to residential back gardens too. This makes getting planning easier than on a greenfield site outside a town. About one third of all new homes built in recent years in London, for example, have been constructed on former residential gardens. The process has become known as 'garden grabbing'.

This is clearly the time to involve your neighbours, as they'll have a view on what goes on in your garden! Whether you get on with them or not, talk to them about your plans. It can be hard to foretell how any one neighbour will respond, so just go for it and see what happens. People get carried away with gossip and fear in such situations. Discuss what you have in mind and see what you can do, even at this early stage, to put their minds at rest and maybe even to enhance their own homes. Most people are pretty decent, especially if they see that your plans could improve the neighbourhood.

The next stage is to talk to a couple of good local estate agents, or an architect or surveyor with experience of similar new-build projects. Ask them what they think of your plans; see what they feel a new house would do to the value of your own home; and get them to estimate what the final value of the new place (and thus the land) could be. It would be very unwise to do anything that would adversely affect your existing home, especially in a poor property market. After all, if you decide to build and live in the new house in your garden you're going to have to sell your existing home to pay for your new build, unless you are very fortunate and can own both homes. If you don't live in the new place but sell it on you'll pay Capital Gains Tax, of course, but this could still make very good financial sense. If you have the resources, it can make sense to build a new house to let as an income. This could be a good move in a failing market when people cannot afford to stay in their homes but could afford to rent. Talk to your estate agent or a surveyor about this particular option.

Getting planning will be your next step. Enrol the help of a local designer who'll advise you what's likely to be possible. A popular route for most people selling their garden is to go for Outline Planning Permission. This simply means that the planners agree that a particular size and type of property is possible on the land but that the final planning permission will be subject to their agreeing to the eventual design details. Getting Outline Planning can be the fastest and best way of releasing cash from your garden. You can then sell the plot on and leave all the worries and building challenges to someone else. Given that you'll already own the land it's unlikely that any other route will produce a better, more stress-free return. It also means you won't have to worry whether you'll be able to sell a new house on the plot, once it's completed. With luck you'll sell your garden with Outline Planning at a high enough price to get you out of financial trouble. This said, when times are hard, the value of your garden as a site will not be as great as it would have been in a buoyant market. Try not to plague yourself with these thoughts but be grateful you've got something to sell and be able to stay in your home.

A major advantage of going the Outline Planning route is that you can impose various restrictive covenants on the land which will ensure that whoever buys it will be unable to ruin your quality of life by building something, or otherwise developing the land, in ways that don't suit you.

Take in another generation

If you have the space it can be a good time to consider taking another generation under your roof. A young adult may, for example, be willing and able to pay for accommodation rather than renting a flat commercially. Millions of families have come to these sorts of arrangements over the years but in recent times young people have expected to rent or buy their own accommodation as soon as possible. When this isn't possible yet they have a good income, it can help both generations to pool resources like this. For the tax implications of this, see below. There's current interest in building a sort of glorified shed in the garden to accommodate a youngster who wants a place of their own. Be sure to get the planning issues on this sorted out before you get too involved.

At the other end of the age scale, how about Granny selling up and coming to live with you? This can make financial sense and also means you can help care for her. Sometimes the deal works both ways, with the grandparent generation helping out with child care. Talk to your IFA about taxation issues. It could be that by selling her home and moving in with you, Granny could settle cash on you to remove it from Inheritance Tax. This might just be the injection you need to keep afloat. This kind of arrangement can be really good when an older person has a home that is too large for them, tying up a lot of capital while their children's generation struggles, or even becomes homeless.

Equity release

These schemes enable those over fifty to get money out of the value of their property while allowing them to live in it. They apply only to those who have no borrowings against their home. There are several different types of scheme with some giving you a regular income, others a lump sum, and yet others, both.

If you go this route you still have to insure your home, telling them of the mortgage lender's or home reversion company's interest in the place. You're expected to keep the place in good repair and could lose it if you don't. The owner of the property could get repairs done and charge them to you or add them to the amount you owe if you don't manage matters properly yourself.

Some schemes forbid certain alterations that could be deemed to lower the value of the place. Check first before doing anything.

Setting up costs can be high. At the time of going to press:

- An arrangement fee was £300 to £600
- A valuation fee about £300
- Legal costs about £500
- Buildings insurance about £250
- Early Repayment Charges varying according to several variables but can be quite costly

All of this means taking legal advice and talking to your IFA before entering into any such arrangement. You'll be given factual information about all schemes in general and about what is being suggested for you in particular.

Two common types of equity release are Lifetime Mortgages and Home Reversion.

Lifetime mortgage (cash release) schemes

With a lifetime mortgage you borrow money but don't have to make any repayments. The amount you can borrow will depend on how old you are and the value of your home. You can take the money out in one lump, or in instalments. Many people use this lump sum to invest in something that produces an income. With this system the lender doesn't own your home but the mortgage must be paid off when you sell, move permanently, or die. You pay interest only on the amount that you owe and this interest is rolled up over the length of the mortgage. Obviously, the longer you live, the greater the interest build-up. Also, it has to be said that this rolling-up of the interest can come to a very large amount of money quite quickly because interest is charged not just on the loan but also on the outstanding interest.

There are both fixed-rate and variable-rate versions of this type of mortgage. It's vital to be sure the mortgage gives you a 'no negative equity guarantee' This ensures you'll never have to pay more than what you get for your home if it is sold for less than the amount you owe.

Home reversion schemes

Home reversion schemes involve you selling a part of your home…which is usually valued pretty low for the purpose because the buyer can't sell the place until you die or move out. The amount you can borrow will depend on your age and your gender. The younger you are and being female (women live longer than men), the less you'll receive. You can remain in your home, even though you don't own it, until the last remaining borrower dies (if you're a couple) or goes into long-term care.

When you die, the place is sold and the reversion company receives their percentage from the proceeds of the sale. The percentage the reversion company gets when your home is sold will depend on the type of contract you have with them. Fixed-share contracts mean their percentage cannot change however long you live or whatever the value of your home at the time of the sale. With a variable-rate contract, the longer you live the less of your property you own. This type of contract gives you more money up-front but the company owns more and more of your home each year. Whatever the contract, the remaining value in your home goes to your named beneficiaries.

Obviously this type of scheme means that should your property rise in value, the company will get a larger amount of money for their fixed percentage share. This said, you or your beneficiaries will also receive an inflated value of the remaining portion.

A really useful website giving information on all this is www.moneymadeclear.fsa.gov.uk

Make money from your home

Let out your home

If you are facing repossession, or fear you might because you're falling behind with your payments, how about letting out your place and moving in with family or friends, or renting a much cheaper place for yourself to live in? You could then use the letting income to pay your mortgage. Of course, you'll have to get enough income from this letting to pay for a home for you to rent, too. Also be aware that by going this route you'll suddenly become a landlord. This brings responsibilities with it such as maintaining the property, providing a rent book if the rent is paid weekly, getting a gas safety certificate, being properly insured, and dealing with your tenants' issues promptly and efficiently. Talk to a solicitor or an advice centre about any of this if you're worried. You'll probably feel more comfortable talking to someone about the legal arrangements anyway, as you'll need to be certain you have the correct type of Rental Agreement with your tenants. The National Landlords Association could also be helpful. Let your insurers know too, as they may raise your premiums.

Tell your lender first then talk to an IFA or Citizen's Advice Bureau about the tax or benefits implications involved. Some lenders will increase your interest rate if you let your place out. Most are open to talks on this, though, especially if it'll enable you to pay them. If you move out for only a short-ish time (say one year) you may be able to claim that your house still remains your principle residence. Much longer than this and the Revenue could say you've become a professional landlord and will thus have to pay Capital Gains Tax when you sell. To be practical for a moment, you may not make a capital gain in a bad market.

But even if you don't have to pay this tax, *income tax* will be due on your letting income. Get professional advice about this as you can claim all kinds of expenses etc against this taxable income.

Choosing a good tenant is the key to success. It might be sensible to go through a professional agency who can take up references and act as a go-between should difficulties arise. If your tenants refuse to pay their rent you can have them evicted but this can be difficult.

Take in a lodger

This can work well if you have a spare room, or even if you could create a spare bed-sit out of a space currently used for something else. Quite a lot of empty-nesters have such spaces, as do some young first-timers. Many people wouldn't consider doing this, except *in extremis*, because they couldn't bear losing their privacy. Others, in contrast, enjoy the company, find the lodger a positive addition to their household, and even make real friends this way.

If you decide to adopt this route you are allowed to make up to £4,250 tax-free a year under the Rent-A-Room Scheme if you live in the same property and the room you let is furnished. You must tell your lender and contents insurance company before doing this. For more information see www.direct.gov.uk

Most lenders will be happy to go along with your plans provided you make it plain how you'll catch up with your missed payments and how you'll fund them in the near future.

In return for your income you'll have to be a good landlord by: looking after the room; getting a valid gas certificate each year; and having an agreement in writing with your lodger before they move in. Your lodger will have to leave if you give reasonable notice but you are not allowed to remove someone physically from your home.

An extension of this could be to give accommodation to a domestic help in exchange for not paying them, or paying them less. Nearly half of all UK households pay for domestic help, so this can be an answer to everyone's needs.

The website SpareRoom.co.uk allows users to advertise free for the first month, after which there is a small charge.

Rent out parking

Parking has now become a seriously valuable asset, especially in town and city centres. If you have a garage that's currently full of junk, or an off-street area that could easily be converted into parking, this could be a good earner with a little effort.

Rent out your second home

More than half a million British people own a second home, whether at home or abroad. When times are good few of them think of their holiday home as a profit centre. However, when cash is tight it a can be a good move to get it rented out. Signs are that about ten percent of second homes will have to be sold as the general property market weakens. But if you can afford to stay put, look carefully at letting. Talk to your lender and insurance company first and take advice about taxation from your IFA as you'll have to pay tax on this income after allowances and expenses.

Short-term holiday lets are most lucrative but are also more aggravation as there's a lot of preparation/

marketing/maintenance involved and more to-ings and fro-ings overall. In general, it's better to go for a long-term let, perhaps with a clause that allows you to use the place for a few weeks a year. If your tenant is using your place as their full-time home and has moved their furniture in, this won't be an option, of course. It will, however, give most comfort to your bank manager or mortgage company, who'll see a constant cash stream.

Renting out your home aboard could be trickier as some low-cost airlines are withdrawing services, thus making access to many people's holiday homes not only more difficult but also more expensive.

Make extra money in other ways

In a book like this I can't go into detail about the many ways you could make cash to keep afloat but things worth considering include:

- Change expensive child care for a live-in 'au pair plus'
- Look for unclaimed assets (such as forgotten insurances, pension, shares, premium bond prizes etc) useful websites include: www.bba.org.uk ; www.bsa.org.uk ; www.thepensionservice.gov.uk; www.uar.co.uk and www.nsandi.com/help/tracemysavings.jsp
- Sell valuable items such a paintings, furniture, jewellery
- Use the services of a pawnbroker
- Do more overtime
- Make a hobby into a home business
- Get a second job
- Direct-sell something from home (such as Avon, Usbourne Books, or Amway)
- Sell a skill (teach someone to play the piano, or book-keeping, for example)
- Sell your main work skill to others on a freelance basis (check with your employer first)
- Pay someone to check that you aren't paying too much tax
- If you are over fifty and have a private pension fund, talk with your IFA about releasing cash from it

Chapter 7
HOW TO INCREASE THE VALUE OF YOUR HOME

When times are hard and you've got to sell, it's vital to make the very best of your home so buyers will choose your house over the twenty-or-so others they'll be viewing. You can do this by enhancing its positive features and minimising the negative ones.

When we set out to buy a house we kid ourselves we're being highly critical and buying rationally but the realities are that most of us buy with our hearts rather than our heads. The sooner you accept this fact the easier it will be to set your sights on exactly what you need to do to sell your property in a difficult market. More than ever now you'll need to get things right, if only because buyers will have a lot of choice and will be being chased by some pretty desperate sellers. I know it's hard but try to put yourself in the eyes of your buyer when preparing your home to sell. If necessary, get a good, honest friend to help with this appraisal. Listen to what they say and don't take things personally. A good friend should feel free to say what has to be said, not what's likely to please you. Such impartial advice can be invaluable, especially if your judgement is impaired because you're stressed or anxious.

The first rule is to remember that you are not selling the house to yourself.

This might seem an odd thing to say but most people want to keep their home exactly as it is and then wonder why it isn't selling. The reason it isn't selling as fast as you'd like – or won't even sell at all in a difficult market – could well be that the way you are presenting it doesn't appeal to your market. And for the purposes of selling, your job is to please the market, not yourself. This could mean making your home look and feel very different from what it usually does. But then your whole task is to appeal to that market. You aren't going to be living in the place for long, so *your* priorities and desires are now a thing of the past.

The minute you put your home on the market you have, in effect, moved out.

Having 'de-loved' your home this much, your challenge is now to 'divorce' it so it can 'get married' to someone else. Many people fail to recognise this basic psychological fact and then wonder why potential buyers can't make the place their own in their mind. At an unconscious level they perceive and feel it is still your 'love' and thus not available for them.

Preparing your home for sale is, therefore, an almost entirely psychological and emotional task as you tailor it to the market in a cold, clinical way that will bring you that sale. However desperate you may be to sell; however hard it is to keep positive about the tiny number of viewings you are getting; however traumatic it is to let the place go, your job is to keep your emotional baggage to yourself and to make your buyer feel good and really keen to buy your place. This can be easier said than done if you're not at your best.

To be able to do this successfully you need to understand the emotional 'business' that's going on in your buyers' minds as *they* look round your home. Although they are being emotional, whatever they claim, you have to stay rationally focused on your task....to put your own emotions to one side and to get the place sold. In a buyers' market when people realise you wouldn't be selling at this stage in the housing cycle unless you had to, you'll find yourself at a disadvantage. This chapter should help redress matters.

Things that put buyers off ... and what to do about them

It is my experience that many people, when viewing properties, are looking for reasons not to buy. This is hugely exaggerated in a poor market where buyers are few and choice is great. The job of the home-owner who has to or wants to sell is thus to ensure that there are as few hurdles as possible for the viewers to jump. In this section I look at what people say puts them off.

Too cluttered

It might seem hypocritical that buyers with cluttered homes of their own are so critical about other people's clutter but it's a fact. There's something especially annoying about other people's clutter. The reason is simple. My clutter is your rubbish! In other words, the things I have around my home that make it uniquely mine and personalise the space to my family, get in the way of a buyer seeing how they could do exactly the same to the place. In a sense, then, your job when presenting your home for sale is to de-personalise it as much as possible so that others can see beyond your world and imagine how they could make it theirs. Down come all those photos of trains; into storage go the hundreds of tatty comics; out go all those holiday knick-knacks, and so on. The principle here is that less is more.

The people who really know how to sell homes are the spec house builders. They spend fortunes on market research, have listened to feedback from their sales-people over many years, and have found from trial and error what sells and what doesn't. This means that the best place for you to start is to go to some show homes. OK, they'll seem like characterless showrooms....and showrooms with small-scale furniture at that – but these sellers cannot afford to get things consistently wrong. Take careful note of what works and what doesn't. Take someone along with you, as you'll be sure to notice different things. Consciously consider why it is that the place looks so inviting….apart from the lack of clutter! Take the best of these tips and apply them to your own place.

When the financial going gets tough, mass-market house builders have to shift their unsold stock or they'll go bust. They will, therefore, be in direct competition with you….and with very much deeper pockets. Learn from their experience and apply it to your house presentation wherever you can. Your very next buyer could have come round the corner from viewing a brand new home, complete with its ten-year guarantee. What will they think about yours? This should be a wake-up call in a tricky market.

Unless you are exceptional, you'll have way too much clutter. Take this opportunity to get rid of stuff you don't need or want and put the rest into store. Remember, you are producing a one-off show house for the market. If you have helpful friends with spare storage, go for this. If not, hire space for a few weeks or months until you're in your new place. This de-cluttering can be very hard and might call from some help. You may have a partner who can make the decisions you find hard, or you may find they are the last person you'd look to in this task. If this is the case, get along a caring friend to assist you in deciding what to keep and what must go. Don't forget I'm not just talking about bits and pieces here. It could be that all kinds of furniture and other large items need to go too. This can be hard if they're of sentimental or emotional significance.

There are many ways of actually getting rid of things.

- Give things to people you know will enjoy or use them
- Have a garage sale, or take stuff to a car-boot sale
- Advertise items in your local paper
- Get proficient on e-Bay (several books are available on Amazon that can help with this), or use an e-Bay selling service
- Give to charities and charity shops
- Get in a valuer if you think something is that special
- Offer things to local voluntary groups
- And when all this is done, hire a skip for the rest

When you're done, the place should look 'bare' by your definition. You should have pared down to things you actually need to live and things that make the place look and 'feel' good. Everything else should have been dumped, given away, sold, or put in store. When de-cluttering, bear in mind the old adage, 'You don't get a second chance to make a first impression'.

Too small

As I know from building and selling houses over the years, the apparent size of a house changes a lot during its construction. And then it changes again in the way it's furnished and presented. Two houses of exactly the same size can look very different in size, according to what's been done to them. In reality you cannot, of course, make your home larger just to sell it (though I look at adding extra space on page 149) but you can do things that make it *appear* bigger.

Things that make houses look bigger include:

- Lots of light/big windows
- Long, uninterrupted, views through the property, preferably out to the back garden

- No clutter
- Small furniture…and not too much of it
- Floor coverings or surfaces that go, uninterrupted, from wall to wall
- Light, neutral wall colours
- High ceilings
- Ceilings that are lighter in colour than the walls
- Flowing, open living spaces (rather than lots of small, interconnected 'boxes')
- A minimum of 'look-at-me' features
- Doors removed to favour arches (house-builders' show homes often have their doors removed!)
- Small (rather than large) paintings etc on walls
- Letting viewers go into small rooms on their own, rather than you going in first and 'filling up' the space

Too dark

Almost everyone says they like a light house. To get the best result:

- Make sure your windows are spotlessly clean inside and out. You'll be amazed what a difference this makes to light levels and also to the feel of the place
- Remove any net curtains or other similar things so the maximum area of glass is exposed. Pull curtains right back off the window. If you're using curtains or blinds to obscure unpleasant outside features be sure they are immaculately clean and tidy
- Make sure all blinds etc are fully up while showing your home
- Unless the day is an exceptionally bright one, have lights on anywhere that's the slightest bit dark
- Give a dark-looking room a coat of light-coloured paint. This can transform it for only a few pounds
- Paint dark ceilings white

- Splash out on some new pale-coloured carpets for dark areas. They don't need to be great quality….it's the effect you're after
- Leave doors open so that dark landings are well-lit

Dirty

There are few things that put people off more than a dirty house. At the simplest level it shows you don't care, which makes them wonder why you don't and colours their view of the place as being *worth* caring for. At another level people ask themselves, 'If the place is so hard for *them* to keep clean, how will *I* manage?'

Rather like our clutter, our dirt is very personal to us. It's all too easy to get used to grimy surfaces; tatty grouting and shower cubicles; dirty floors and stained carpets, and stuff lying around the place and still find the place perfectly liveable. But then your task isn't to sell to yourself!

There's no excuse for your home being dirty. Keep it spotlessly clean and tidy the whole time it's on the market, if only because that all-important buyer might turn up at a moment's notice. This has happened to me on several occasions!

Too old or too new

There's not much you can do about the age of your home, when selling. However, you can make life easier for your potential buyer. The crucial thing is not to confuse. People looking at period houses expect and want to see period features. The same principle applies to contemporary homes. If you confuse people they find it hard to see the really good features you're offering. Although it's possible to combine the best of the old with the best of the new, be sure you're doing this with style or it will lose you sales.

- Make the most of your period features
- Get rid of, or store, items that are out of place in the overall style of your home
- Be sure that things that upset people about older homes are attended to. These include: damp; bad roofing; poor exterior decoration; doors and windows that don't work properly or are in poor repair; and out-dated plumbing and electrics. If you're offering your place as a fixer-upper you will take a different view on all this, but this won't usually be the case

Needs too much maintenance

Most people today say they want to spend the minimum amount of time and energy maintaining their homes. This is why items such as swimming pools are so unpopular with buyers. With a pool, vendors see a fun family resource – potential buyers, nothing but bills and aggravation. Similarly, uPVC windows and doors are popular because they need almost no maintenance, even over many years. Paying people to maintain things is so expensive that most buyers don't want to take on anything that looks like costing them dearly in the future.

Though you may not be able, or willing, to refurbish your home (outside or in) to remove all high-maintenance materials and features, you certainly can and must ensure that everything like this is in tip-top working order and maintained to the highest level. This goes for gardens, too of course. If high-maintenance items appear effortless to your buyers they might just overlook them in the heat of the moment while they focus on other features of your home. But anything that stands out as needing attention is a poisoned chalice they dare not grasp, especially if they are concerned about their future finances, as many people are in an economic downturn.

Maintenance is an especially important issue when selling a flat. If it's in a large block or development your buyer will end up paying for a share of the maintenance expenses on the whole property – and these can be very considerable if, say, the roof needs replacing or the driveways and parking areas need resurfacing. Do all the homework you can to help inform buyers about future possible outgoings on major projects. Give all the good news you can: 'We had the garage roofs all done last year, and a re-paint two years ago'.

In summary; if your property comes across as difficult for *you* to maintain, rest assured your buyers will fear they too will be unable to do so.

Badly-done DIY

According to one survey, ninety per cent of people looking round houses are put off by poor DIY efforts. This is hardly surprising, given that if things look bad on the surface you can be pretty certain what's hidden will be even worse! This is especially likely to put buyers off in a time of financial uncertainty when the last thing they'll want is a nasty expense for something that the seller bodged the year before selling. If you're working harder, trying to find work or making efforts to live on a reduced income the last thing you'll want is someone else's DIY disasters.

Lacks privacy

People's ideas of privacy, and indeed the need for it, differ hugely. To one buyer, the fact that your garden is overlooked by the neighbours will pose no problem, whilst to another it could be a deal-breaker. This said, it makes sense to have an area somewhere around the house where you can sit or sunbathe privately. The place may not be all that private *sound-wise* but most people living among others are prepared to accept this.

Cast your mind back to what other people have said about your home over the years, and listen to what estate agents say when valuing the place. I think it's important to actually ask estate agents what they think could be done to make your home more attractive. Remedy anything you can and then relax about it.

No storage

Most modern homes have far too little storage. For reasons that are beyond me, even very able architects seem to place too little value on storage space, yet people constantly complain there isn't enough. The result is that most of those with a loft or garage use one or both for storage. Few people today keep cars in their garages.

One way of overcoming this problem when trying to sell is to de-clutter, so buyers don't even imagine there's no storage. By getting rid of stuff, you could find that your existing storage does well enough, or that a few pounds spent at somewhere such as IKEA could solve your problems elegantly. If you have storage, be sure to point it out. If you don't, for the purposes of selling, put stuff into rented, commercial storage and out of your viewer's sight!

Garden too big or too small

Over the last twenty years or so most people have changed their lifestyle in ways that preclude spending much time maintaining a garden. If you have a wonderful garden, this feature will attract a particular type of buyer. But if your garden isn't that great, go out of your way to show it isn't a liability. Anyway, whatever state it's in, be sure to display it at its best when buyers come. Whatever you do you won't be able to please everyone. And many buyers are fickle when it comes to gardens. I've found that some people who swear a garden is too big and they'll put it all down to decks and gravel, in fact end up becoming green-fingered. The reverse also occurs.

Too noisy

People's views on noise differ greatly. Some seem to be able to hear a cat peeing two gardens away and others actually like the sound of the neighbour's children playing. There's no accounting for taste. A busy road will be all too obvious to your buyers – and will put many off. Planting a stout hedge at the front can mask a lot of this and the price will usually reflect the noisy location anyway. Noisy neighbours or planes can, though, be impossible to do anything about.

Once in the house you can control things better. Good-quality double, or even triple, glazing not only helps conserve heat but is very effective at keeping noise out. When viewers ask about noise I think it's wise to be honest but not to overplay it. I was once selling a country house a mile from a busy motorway. I mentioned the noise to one buyer, pointing out that in the wet weather it was pretty obvious, only to be told that, compared with where they currently lived, the place was like a morgue! Noise, like so many things to do with people's homes, is a very subjective issue. On the other side of this coin, it pays to remember that we all become used to ambient noise levels. Those who live near railway tracks simply don't hear the trains. I was once searching for a property close to a major airport. When viewing houses there I noticed that vendors simply stopped talking while a plane went overhead. When I pointed this out to them they said they hadn't realised they were doing it....and that the noise didn't bother them, either.

And noise isn't 'noise' to everyone. We all have our individual ideas about what we find unacceptably noisy yet to others this sound can be pleasant or even reassuring. One house I sold was unsellable for a time because some buyers said they couldn't stand the silence! Some older people say they like a degree of noise so they don't feel too cut off from neighbours, for example.

Noise doesn't travel in straight lines, remember! It can bounce off, or be muffled by, other local buildings, which can mean that one house in an area can be noisy (say from a train line) whereas another quite close by may not be. This muffling can vary greatly, according to the weather, too.

Time of day can be important too, when showing a home that could be noisy. Obviously, if you live near a football ground you won't choose to show on Saturday afternoons!

Too expensive

Everyone wants a great house for little money, so price is often a reason people give for not wanting a buy. Bear in mind that people often use price to disguise, or be polite about, issues that have nothing at all to do with money.

Bad first impression

There's an old saying in property circles: first impressions are lasting impressions. And how true this is. I look below at how to get those vital first impressions right.

Bad layout

I'd like a pound for every time I've heard people say how good a house was but what a pity it was spoilt by its room layout. This isn't necessarily something you'd be prepared to tackle in a need-to-sell moment but it can make a vast difference if you have time to take a longer view.

Get an architect, or other design professional, or a good local estate agent to come and look at your layout. You could be surprised that for a relatively small amount of money you could re-model the place to make a big difference to its saleability. People today want large eat-in kitchen/family rooms; en-suite bathrooms; converted lofts; and smaller numbers of open spaces rather than many small boxes. I know it might sound like a lot of work and disruption but it could make all the difference between a sale and a very long wait. If there's a similar house in your street that's been improved like this, then unless you're aiming to sell to a builder or developer (cheaply!) you'll find it hard to attract a buyer. In troubled times, most people will want to buy somewhere they can put their things and get on with their lives. In your favour is the fact that when the market is tough there are lots of builders around who'll be grateful for the work. They'll not only be available but will give you a good price.

The best way to think about all this is to get out there viewing houses that are like yours in your neighbourhood. See what other people have done, talk to local agents and work out what this has done to their asking price or saleability. I know it'll sound counter-intuitive but you may just have to spend to sell. Never be tempted to over-spend in a failing market, though, and be sure not to over-personalise in your efforts to attract a buyer.

Bad neighbours

This is a tricky subject that is another highly subjective issue. To one particular individual a neighbour may be 'impossible', yet to another, 'ideal'. It'll depend entirely on what you think is acceptable or desirable in a neighbour. One person's 'nosey' is another's 'welcome concern and interest'. If you've had a serious dispute with a neighbour you have to declare it to your solicitor before selling but few people have this level of problem. Issues such as caravans or work vans parked next to your driveway or in front of your home really cannot be legislated for. It's all very well asking your neighbour if he'll take it away while you're showing the place but people will be driving by for many weeks or even months, so this won't usually be practical, however helpful your neighbour.

When buying a flat, a lot of people ask the neighbours what it's like living there. You'll be amazed how loose-tongued some people will be when asked outright!

Ways of adding value

Research shows that, in general, the best ways of adding value to your home are (in this order):

- Sorting out problems that affect the whole or part of the house (for example, a leaking roof/damp/cracks/central heating/double glazing etc)
- Adding more living/bedroom/home office space by converting a loft or garage (you already have the space)
- A new kitchen
- Updating the decorations in neutral colours
- Adding more ground floor space with an extension
- A new bathroom
- Off-road parking
- Insulation to enhance the energy rating of your home

Things that are a waste of money in a poor market include:

- Gadgets and toys (flat-screen TVs and home cinemas, for example)
- Jacuzzis and hot tubs
- Swimming pools and saunas
- Home gyms
- Any highly-personalised architectural or decorative features
- Roof terraces and balconies
- Anything that's expensive to maintain

Things that actually put people off buying include:

- Taking out period features (fireplaces, decorative plasterwork, nice old doors etc)
- Stone cladding

- Building work that drastically reduces the size of the garden
- Plastic windows in a period house
- The only bathroom being downstairs

Preparing to show your home - room by room

Once your home is on the market it must be kept in viewable condition for the whole time. In a poor market, viewers are likely to be few and far between. This means that each and every one of them will be more important to you than in a buoyant market. Given that your new job of work is to get your house sold, keeping everything ready for viewing is a vital part of that task.

Kerb appeal

However brilliant your house is inside, unless you get people over the threshold, they'll never know. The first impression your buyers will get is of the outside. Whether you like it or not, this is how many will judge the entire place. When there's a lot of choice, buyers will simply drive by if they don't like what they see.

- Make sure your house name or number is clear. There's no worse a start than viewers arriving late and frustrated because they couldn't find you
- Tidy up the front path. Make sure there are no roots, weeds or other stuff that people could fall over. If your paving needs attention, spend some cash to sort it out. This needn't mean new pathways
- Get rid of any junk/bikes/rubbish bins and so on
- Trim hedges and lawns. It makes sense to fertilise your front lawn regularly to keep it looking green. Plant a few pounds' worth of colourful flowers, if they're in season. This will brighten things up at a stroke
- Check that all light fittings are in good order and work. A buyer stumbling around in the dark starts off in a bad mood

- If your front door is dated or tatty, find cash to replace it
- Check that curtains and blinds are drawn back to look attractive. The windows are the eyes of your home and people want to be able to see them clearly
- If your exterior paintwork is past its sell-by date, repaint
- Are your front garden boundaries in good order? Could a few cheap fence panels liven things up a bit?
- If you have a pet, see that there are no poos anywhere in the front. Soiled shoes on your flooring is a bad start to a viewing
- Hose down or pressure-wash your driveway. If at all possible, get rid of cars on viewing days so people can easily park outside
- If it's icy, put down some salt on paths and drives to make your buyers feel safe as they approach your home
- Get out into the street and clear up any obvious litter in the area immediately around your place
- Remove dead plants and tidy up flower beds. Have a good weed and perhaps cover up the open earth with a commercial mulch such as wood chippings
- Trim any overhanging braches of trees so viewers don't have to fight their way through an obstacle course
- Next time it's raining hard, go outside and check that your gutters aren't overflowing and that down-pipes are doing what they should. Get them fixed if they need attention

Kitchen
Often a deal-breaker, especially for women.

- Make sure everywhere and everything is spotlessly clean
- Clear away all kitchen appliances that aren't actually being used
- There should be no evidence of washing up

- Clean that oven. You'd be surprised how many buyers casually open a kitchen appliance and cupboard doors – it's as if it's a mindless reflex
- Remove everything you can from work-tops so they appear large and useable
- Clean the extractor fan and its filters so that it functions really well. You'll be using this to ensure your kitchen doesn't smell unpleasant before buyers come around
- Put out clean hand towels and tea towels
- Get rid of anything on the floor that shouldn't be there. This makes the floor area look as large as possible
- Rubbish bins and recycling bins should be empty
- Check that the door to the garden works as it should
- Have some coffee brewing for its feel-good aroma
- If you can't make your silicone seals around work tops etc look clean, cut them out and replace them

Bedrooms

- Make sure all beds are made and pillows etc, tidy
- Remove all clutter and things lying around on the floor
- Vacuum the floor
- Look carefully at traffic areas to see that furniture doesn't obstruct your path. We all get used to this as a norm we live with but it creates a very bad impression for someone new to the property. Don't forget there could be several people, including your agent, going into a room at one time
- Ensure that laundry baskets etc are shut and not over-brimming
- Organise wardrobes and dressing rooms so the clothes look neat. There's no point having great wardrobes if people feel embarrassed about peaking in to them
- Clean mirrors and TV screens
- Check there are no loose TV, computer, telephone or extension cables lying around to trip people up

Bathrooms and loos

- All bathrooms and loos should shine
- Check for dripping taps and showers and plugholes that don't drain as they should. Clean hairs etc out of plugholes
- Clean that grouting between tiles. If you can't get caulking (silicones) to look good, cut them out and replace them
- Make sure all visible towels are fresh and clean
- Buy a nice plant for a strategic position
- Have a prominently-placed hand towel in your bathroom or cloakroom for use by your viewers, should they need one
- Make sure all loos smell fresh before a viewing. Open the windows for a few minutes before people come, to let that fresh air in
- Keep loo-seat covers down when showing your home and tidy the loo paper roll

Other rooms

- Vacuum and dust everywhere
- Clean up toys, junk, clothes, and any plants that don't look great. Buy some simple plants or flowers to brighten the place up
- Check that every door and window works properly. People will soon discover that a door or window sticks or won't close as they pull it to
- Give the walls a fresh lick of paint, if necessary
- If it's cold outside, light the fire. This not only shows it works but is also welcoming
- Light any areas that are the slightest bit dark
- Make sure the house feels pleasantly warm
- Be aware that placing furniture opposite a fireplace, or other similar feature, can make the room appear very narrow and reduce circulation space

- If you have a pet, ask a friend to come round and tell you if they think your home smells. If it does then get carpets cleaned or replace them if necessary. On the day of a viewing it makes sense to leave your dog with a neighbour or friend, if you can. Many people are immediately put off a house because of pet smells, or the unwanted attentions of your pooch!

Outside areas

- Clear up everywhere
- Get rid of dead or not-so-great-looking plants and shrubs
- Mow lawns and trim edges and hedges. Keep your lawn well fertilised so it looks green all year round
- Weed-kill pathways
- Get your boundary fences etc looking the best you can. If necessary, renew them. Many people are very keen on boundaries and like to see where their property begins and ends
- Check that steps are safe. Repair them, if necessary
- Make sure that patio is hosed down or pressure-hosed to make it sparkle. Unless your barbecue looks the part, dump it. Do the same with any garden furniture. When selling your outdoor space, remember to think of it as another 'room' that should add to the lifestyle you are selling. Do whatever you reasonably can to be sure this is happening
- Get some colourful plants and flowers in season to brighten up the place

Information is power

Over the years I have viewed literally hundreds of houses. It never ceases to amaze me how often the owner is ignorant of even quite basic things about their home that are of interest to me as a potential buyer.

It should be your task to have everything imaginable available at your fingertips. It is in most people's nature to fear that a lack of knowledge or information is being used to conceal something nasty. If they don't think this, then at the very least the not-knowing could fuel unconscious fears. The truth is that once a potential buyer starts to fear something they'll create conscious or unconscious barriers to your home that could take ages (and/or lots of money) to overcome. A simple, confident answer, timely given, smoothes a buyer's decision-making. What you don't want is for your home to stand out among those they see *for the wrong reason*.

If a couple are viewing several properties in a day they'll remember each one for different things. Your task is to ensure that yours sticks out in their memories for the best possible reasons. All too often I hear people describing a house as, 'You know, that one with the tatty roof'. The rest of the place could have been great but in a buyers' market this single feature could make all the difference. If the owner could confidently say, 'We've had the roof looked at and the company says it's just a few loose slates. We're getting them fixed as soon as the weather picks up', the matter would be done and dusted there and then.

During the twenty years I practised as a psychotherapist I dealt every day with people's questions. I also, at one stage of my life, trained sales teams. Even an apparently simple enquiry can hide a multitude of hidden agendas. It's your job when selling to discover what that agenda is and to try to put your buyer's mind at rest so they'll keep going and buy your home.

In order to do this you may need to ask some gentle questions about who will be living in the place, if they were to buy. Knowing about children, an elderly relative, or someone with a disability, for example, could all help you pitch your sale more accurately, and helpfully.

For example, your buyer may ask what the parking is like in the road. A good reply might be, 'What is your main concern?' After all, they're not looking to you to become a town planner and deliver a lecture on urban parking issues in your borough! This answering of their question with a question usually brings out the actual concern. 'At our last place we often had to park two streets away and drag the push chair and shopping around in the rain. It wasn't great. In fact, it's one of the reasons we're moving'. Suddenly you're in a good position to give information that really means something to your buyer. You've moved your sale forward in a positive way. Even if your answer isn't exactly what they want to hear, you could still be better off getting the issue out in the open and then leaving it to the buyer to decide if it's a deal-breaker for them. Human nature abhors an information vacuum. By filling it, even with a less-than-perfect answer you'll keep your buyer in the game.

Questions to which you should have full, and preferably insightful, answers include:

- How long have you been on the market?
- Is the place freehold or leasehold?

- Are you in a chain and when do you want to move?
- What is the area like to live in?
- What are the neighbours like?
- Have you ever had any problems with them?
- Where is the nearest train station/bus etc? How long does it take to walk there? They won't want to hear you've never walked because you always go by car!
- Where are the nearest schools? Are they any good?
- Where do you send your children to school?
- What's the area like for crime?
- Have you ever been burgled?
- What sort of security measure have you got?
- What's the road like during rush hours?
- What's the parking like in the road?
- How close are the nearest shops?
- Is there a kids' playground nearby?
- Where could I walk my dog?
- What do you most like about living in the road/area?
- What's the area like for pubs and restaurants?
- Are you staying local?
- What have you done to the place since you've lived here?
- Have you had the place re-wired/re-plumbed?
- Is the conservatory still under guarantee?
- Would it be possible to convert the loft?
- What have you done about energy saving?
- How much are your utility bills and council tax? It's sensible to have some recent bills available for inspection
- What's the internet like here?
- When was the roof last re-done?
- What sort of heating have you got? Is it effective? Who services it?
- What fixtures and fittings did you intend leaving?
- If you're selling a flat in a block or conversion: What's

the ground rent and service charge? What's the management company like? How good are the other residents about getting things done? Is there a resident's association? How good is it? What complaints have you got about the block?

- Why are you moving? It's important here to have positive, plausible reasons even if they aren't completely accurate. Property professionals say there are always two reasons why people sell….the reason they give and the real reason! People don't want to hear about your impending bankruptcy or divorce but will understand most family/job-related reasons. Or you could say you want a bigger garden/to move to the coast/be closer to your children's' schools, etc. Most buyers in a bad market will be only too aware that financial hardship will be near the top of your list but this can simply be hinted at. Whatever reason you give, it mustn't smell of desperation or your buyers will know they can go in for the kill. Definitely stay away from negative reasons, such as complaints about the inaccessibility of the local shops; death; divorce; or expensive pubs and restaurants!

Chapter 8
BUYING A HOME

People were buying houses in their thousands every day of the week (about 1.2 million a year in the UK in 2007) but in this property downturn this number is probably about halved. I'm looking at buying, here, because there are many who have never thought they'd need to move home and who are out of touch with what's involved. In this section I look at how to buy your new home, the stages involved, and how things are different in a property downturn.

What can you afford?

This is the first stage in your buying process. There's absolutely no point going out looking at places until you have completed this stage. Go through your finances very carefully, even perhaps with help from an IFA if you have one, or an adviser at the Citizen's Advice Bureau. In the present climate when lenders are being cautious and rationing mortgages, buyers with a genuine mortgage offer will have a distinct negotiating advantage over those that don't. Now is the time to be very realistic. Look especially at:

- All your savings, investments and cash at the bank, bearing in mind that they may be worth much less than you thought

- How much you are earning – remembering that you'll need to be totally realistic about how safe your job is
- How much equity you have in your home (get two or three estate agents or a surveyor to value your place first)
- Any other possible sources of cash (parents, other relatives, selling anything valuable you don't need or want)
- What your regular commitments are, apart from your mortgage

Next, make out a list of all the expenses involved in buying (see page 207) and selling (see page 138). There are lots of odd costs that can mount up alarmingly quickly. The total of this list will have to be taken into account when looking at what you can afford.

I won't give any actual costs here because things vary according to: where you live in the country; changing Government policy (especially on taxes); what professionals will charge (when they need the work); and even what it costs to move house (when removal companies will be competing heavily for your business).

Buying costs

Buying costs to be aware of include:

A survey fee
Your new place will need surveying if you want to borrow someone else's money to pay for it. And you may well want a survey even if it's your own cash you're using. Talk to a local surveyor about what he'll charge and the type of report you'll want. This will depend to some extent on the age and condition of the place; how large a mortgage you'll need; and various other things. Get two surveyors to quote on this.

Valuation fees
Your lender may require you to get the place valued, or they'll have it done then charge you. This usually comes to a few hundred pounds.

Stamp Duty
This is a sort of purchase tax you pay when buying a house. It kicks in at £175,000 at the time of going to press. The amount payable escalates with the price of the house. Reducing levels of Stamp Duty is something governments can do to ease the burden on buyers, especially first-time buyers who are struggling to get into the market. Unfortunately, in a property downturn, governments are strapped for cash like the rest of us and are loath to reduce their tax take. It has been calculated that suspending Stamp Duty for one year on all properties up to £250,000 would lose the exchequer somewhere around £3 billion.

The intrinsic inequity of Stamp Duty as a tax is all the more unpleasant because the numbers of first-time buyers paying higher-rate Stamp Duty doubled over the years 2006-2008. Given the UK government's aim to encourage young people to own their own homes, this cannot be sensible.

This said, in this troubled market such as today's, enticing first-time buyers to embark on a house purchase by offering them, on average, a £1,800 tax 'gift' (and perhaps only a suspended one), could be said to be irresponsible. In fact, a survey in mid-2008 found that 80% of first-timers said they wouldn't see such a suspension or abolition of Stamp Duty as an incentive to buy. Someone I know brought their asking price down to below the £175,000 level, only to discover that despite lots of interest, no-one could actually raise the cash.

The Conservative Government in the UK gave the depressed property market in the early 1990s a kick-start by suspending Stamp Duty for a time. It worked for a while but when it was re-introduced the property downturn came back to bite them.

A later treasury analysis of the 1991 decision reported that, 'Once the duty was re-imposed, the number of transactions collapsed and prices fell sharply….So the Stamp Duty holiday, which had been intended to bring forward a recovery in the housing market, ended up further undermining the confidence that was essential to recovery'.

In fact, Stamp Duty is a very unfair tax overall. Unlike other taxes, it is charged at the highest appropriate rate on the whole sale price, including those parts below the thresholds. There is a case to be made for paying it only on the difference in price between what we are buying and what we are selling. The lower threshold needs raising too (arguably to £250,000) in view of such high house prices.

Stamp Duty rates at the time of going to press were:

- Up to £125,000 nil (£175,000 for one year from September 2008)
- £125,000 to £250,000 1%
- £250,000 to £500,000 3%
- £500,000 upwards 4%

Useful information can also be found at www.hmrc.gov.uk/so

If you live in a 'disadvantaged area' you could get Stamp Duty relief up to £175,000. For details on whether this could apply to you, go to http://www.hmrc.gov.uk/so/dar/dar-search.htm

Housing Finance is an on-line journal that covers mortgage-related topics. Non-members can get access to all kinds of useful information free on www.cml.org.uk/cml/statistics

Land Registry fee

Your solicitor or conveyancer will organise this. It costs only a few pounds.

Local authority search fees

When buying a property you'll need to know what the local authority will charge you for any outstanding or on-going services. This document search, carried out by your solicitor or conveyancer, will discover if there are any restrictions, decisions or information, or even outstanding financial claims on the property. This will show, for example, any restrictions or conditions placed on planning permissions; charges for roads; and matters to do with tree preservation orders, listed buildings and conservation areas.

This search costs very little money and is a vital part of the investigation of your proposed home. No solicitor or conveyancer will let you buy without such a search.

Lender's fees

Anyone who arranges a mortgage for you can charge you for their services. Be certain you ask exactly how much these fees will come to when talking to lenders, brokers, IFAs, or whomever. Ask whether there'll be a higher lending charge (HLC) too.

Home Information Pack (HIP)

The cost of this is borne by the seller but you might have to pay for copying and mailing.

Removal expenses

Although there'll be good deals to be done, with so many removal companies going to the wall, make your bill lighter still by getting rid of everything you possibly can before you move. If you're down-sizing you'll need to do this anyway. But there's no sense paying for the removal of stuff you'll then end up selling, or throwing away.

Storage expenses

If you can't move directly from one house to another, you'll find that storage can amount to quite an expense. Get several quotes. It's usually best to use the people who remove you to store things temporarily (perhaps while you rent, if this is the route you are going). Be very careful about what you store. Get rid of everything you possibly can – no matter how hard it seems at the time.

There are few things more depressing than getting loads of stuff out of store, that's cost you a small fortune to keep there, only to discover that you really don't want it.

Unpaid bills and other debt

Any bills, or even debts, that are linked to your current home will have to paid off before starting with a clean slate on your new place. Some lenders, under normal circumstances, will let you take debts against your home across to new borrowings with them. Under current circumstances, though, this is increasingly unlikely. Be sure to get this clarified with your proposed lender.

Legal fees

Although it is possible for you, personally, to handle all the legal issues involved in buying and selling, I advise you not to do so. Especially when the market is tough, it's vital not to make mistakes. A solicitor or a conveyancing company will know all the wrinkles and help you stay safe in a dangerous property climate. Quickly-bought 'bargains', for example, can catch out even seasoned professionals. Just because times are tough, shouldn't make you any less careful about legal matters. In fact the contrary could be the case as sellers get desperate to off-load property and may be tempted to mis-represent things, or cut legal corners.

Running costs of your new home

If finances are going to be tight once you've moved, be sure to have a realistic handle on what your future outgoings are likely to be. Your mortgage repayments will probably be the biggest single outgoing but also think of:
- Heating/energy bills
- Community charges or council taxes
- Water rates
- Ground rent (for leasehold properties)
- Service charges (if your new place is a leasehold property; bearing in mind that these charges rise over the years)
- Insurance premiums

- Payments for buying your car etc
- Servicing any other loans or debts you have that aren't linked to your home's value. Many people take selling as an opportunity to get out of the huge interest payments involved in credit card debt, for example. This is a good time to take stock of your finances in general. If you're moving because you've got cash problems, the last thing you want is to dig yourself into trouble again within a couple of years
- Contributions to a private pension fund
- Life insurance policies you may have
- Any necessary improvements you'll have to make to the new place in the first year
- School/college/university fees
- Any family commitments you've undertaken (for example, supporting children through college or university, looking after aged relatives etc). Don't forget to look ahead on this sort of thing. You may not have these kinds of outgoings today but could they become a drain in the foreseeable future? Unless you want to move again when things get tight, it pays to think this through now and plan what you can afford on your new home

In summary:
On a £200,000 property:

Assuming you're paying only a five per cent deposit (which will be a very hard deal to strike these days, it'll be more likely to be ten per cent, or even much more) you need to include Stamp Duty; legal costs; local searches and Land Registry fees; a mortgage arrangement fee; a lender's valuation fee; your mortgage broker's fee (if you use one); and a survey. All these will bring costs alone to about £17,000 at late 2008 prices. And this won't include all the other items I listed above. Pay a 20% deposit and then add removal and storage costs and you're soon looking at £50,000 before spending a penny on doing anything to your new place!

I hope this shows just how realistic you need to be when thinking about moving. And if you also have something to sell, there'll be selling costs to bear as well (see page 138). When financial times are tight, it can make good sense to stay put for cash reasons alone, whatever other motives you have for moving.

First-time buyers

First-time buyers are having an especially hard time at the moment. Not only are they in the middle of a housing crisis that is making even seasoned home-buyers flinch, but the uncertainty they face is great. The government announced a rescue package in September 2008, aimed at helping first-timers take that first step on to the property ladder.

It consisted of two parts:

The first was a twelve-month holiday from Stamp Duty, allowing purchasers of properties up to £175,000 to be exempt from paying the 1% duty that had until then been levied on properties costing more than £125,000. In reality, though, this is a token that does little to help first-timers as, at best, it will save them only £1,750, which is a small sum in the scheme of normal buying costs (somewhere between £20,000 and £30,000). And such a tiny sum could anyway be very quickly erased by falling values. I think any efforts by the government to entice young people into this current, hazardous market should be treated with extreme caution, it is even seen by some as being irresponsible.

The second part of the plan was to introduce a shared-equity scheme in which the government and house-builders would lend first-timers up to 30% of the value of their property interest-free for five years. The remaining 70% has to be obtained from a lender, savings, parents, or all three.

Parents have often been a good source of cash for first-time buyers but in an uncertain financial climate this strategy is becoming very risky. Many parents are finding it hard to keep their own heads above water, let alone take on further debt, or even act as guarantors for their children's debts. This said, more than £27 billion has been invested by parents in their children's properties over recent years and most parents who can, still want to help.

The government's new shared equity scheme, known as Homebuy Direct, is available only to 10,000 first-time buyers with a household income of less than £60,000. They can use this scheme only for new-build properties. Of about a third of a million first-time buyers each year, these conditions apply to only a tiny fraction. There are other, better, shared-equity loan schemes around. Talk to a professional about them. Some such methods of buying allow you to purchase a larger stake in your home when you can afford to, so you can pay back some, or even all, of the loan. Some shared-equity schemes have built-in negative equity protection. Another interesting system is a sort of 'try-before-you-buy' setup. In one such arrangement you can rent for up to two years before deciding to buy. You can then count up to one year's paid rent as a deposit.

Shared-ownership schemes aren't new, of course. There have, for a long time, been all manner of ways of buying only a fraction of a property, perhaps paying rent on the rest and even buying a larger share as time goes by and funds permit. The owners of such properties are usually local authorities or housing associations, though mass-market house-builders are now offering similar opportunities. Private builders' schemes sell the property at a discount, enabling buyers to pay a lower mortgage and make up the rest as rent. It's vital to be aware that any discounts can be quickly swallowed up in a falling market and that whatever such companies claim, they are in business for the benefit of their share-holders – not for that of first-time buyers. If a deal seems too good to be true - it probably is!

As time goes by in this difficult market, all kinds of innovative schemes will be devised to help first-time buyers. In my opinion they all need careful scrutiny because they could lure young people into a falling market that could damage their financial future, should they find themselves repossessed, or worse. As always in the property market, if something seems too good to be true, it probably is! The world of estate agents, government spin doctors, lenders, and all manner of other property professionals is crazy to create activity in the market in these dire conditions, so they themselves can survive.

In my view, this is a time for extreme caution - especially if you're a first-time buyer. If in any doubt, sit tight until the dust settles.

Mortgages

A mortgage is simply a method by which you can borrow money to buy a home. At the family level you could get the cash from a rich uncle, but most of us find ourselves dealing with the vast industry that does this sort of lending every day. There are about twelve million current mortgages in the UK, and they are available from several sources:

- Banks
- Building societies
- Finance houses
- Insurance companies (mainly endowment mortgages which are now unpopular and uncommon)
- Specialist mortgage companies
- Private individuals (a relative, for example, can give you a loan to buy your home)
- Special 'sub-prime' mortgage companies that give loans to those who would otherwise find it difficult or impossible to raise money elsewhere because of, for example, bankruptcy; County Court Judgments; previous repossession; etc)

I'm a fan of professional advisers and reckon it's worth talking to a mortgage broker/adviser, or an independent financial adviser, if you have one, from the start. This is a particularly helpful route if your mortgage is in any way unusual. It may, for example, be that you're looking for a very large loan, or that your proposed property is special in some way. There are about 30,000 mortgage brokers in the UK but their numbers are falling fast. If you want to buy with others or are self-employed with an unstable income, an experienced helper can be very useful. Take care when selecting one – ideally, go by personal recommendation.

If you're a Muslim, you might need an Islamic mortgage. In this case, Sharia law forbids the charging or receiving of interest, so you'll pay your lender a 'rent' instead. An interesting principle that underlies all property transactions governed by Sharia law is that any return on funds provided by a Muslim financier can be earned only by way of profit derived from a commercial risk taken by the financier. In other words, money cannot simply be used to make money. Looked at philosophically this is a very attractive proposition.

If you have any difficulty finding a broker, look in the *Yellow Pages* or talk to the Citizen's Advice Bureau. A good broker could prevent you from losing your valuation fee. Some of the larger agents such as John Charcol (www.charcolonline.co.uk) are authorised to appoint a valuer, so if the valuation comes in below the agreed price and your original lender won't play ball, you can use this valuation to go to another lender.

But you don't have to get your mortgage through a professional adviser – it's possible to go direct to lenders and save money. Things have recently changed on this. Until some time in 2007 lenders were more than happy for brokers to do a lot of the work on finding them business. A broker might have earned a fee of 0.3% of the loan value. With the financial conditions that prevail today, lenders are keen to have customers deal with them directly. In fact, many of the best deals are to be had *only* direct from lenders themselves.

Saving money like this could be important if you're in financial straits. This said, the mortgage world is full of smoke and mirrors and it's good to have someone on your side to help you chart your way through the maze unless you are pretty financially aware or your needs and financial situation are simple. Also, by going to a single lender they'll tell you only about *their* products, whereas a broker will have his finger on many and could choose the one that's best for your circumstances. In a normal market a good broker would have about 15,000 products from more than 100 lenders at his fingertips. Today, with the current mortgage problems, the number of products has fallen to about 4,500. Price comparison sites on the internet can be helpful when making a choice but even the Financial Services Authority's own site can sometimes be out of date.

Obviously, nothing written in this book can be taken as advice to any individual reader: such advice can be given only by those who are authorised by the Financial Services Authority (FSA) or the Council of Mortgage Lenders. Indeed, even the advice you receive from a professional needs to be considered very carefully. Many people claim that they took out the size of mortgage they did because they felt their mortgage adviser, by offering it, knew what he was talking about. The ultimate responsibility is yours, and no one else's. The experts aren't going to pay your mortgage for you! A 2008 study done by the Consumers Association in Britain found that a substantial minority of mortgage advisers actually gave rather poor advice, especially when it came to affordability.

At this time of uncertainty in the property market, it's vital to bear in mind that your home may be at risk if you don't keep up the payments on your borrowings. We all tend to gloss over this statement in the not-so-small print when times are good but now the market has gone downhill, it's plain that countless individuals didn't give this warning the consideration it deserved. Amazingly, about one in ten people, according to one poll, say that they have never read their mortgage agreement! I bet the real figure is higher.

The business of selling mortgages is highly regulated. Since October 2004 it has been regulated by the Financial Services Authority. People selling you a mortgage have to tell you how they are qualified to do so and must say if they are independent or linked to a particular bank/mortgage/insurance company. They also have to declare how they get paid. Some will charge you by the hour, others a percentage of the loan, and yet others nothing at all if they are getting paid by the lender. Each of these has its advantages and disadvantages but as long as you know what's going on, you should be able to ask the right questions. Mortgage brokers have, traditionally, been good sources of information and personal service for those getting a mortgage. As the industry is changing because of the current downturn, many lending organisations are cutting down the commissions they pay their agents or brokers and some are even cutting out brokers altogether. They argue that they can give a better service this way but, in reality, a middle man is just another cost they can do without when times are tough for them.

Just how much a lender will offer you will vary according to many things. In recent buoyant markets lenders have been over-keen to throw money at borrowers in an effort to make the most profit they can. However, in a declining property market, lenders are finding they are neither prepared to take the risk this involves, nor can they lay their hands on enough cash by borrowing from other financial institutions. It isn't widely known that even very big banks get their cash to lend to the public from other lending sources. All these institutions lend to one another. In the last year or so, even very large outfits have been caught with bad debts and repossessions and so have tended to hoard their cash rather than lend it to others to re-lend. This has led to a severe shortage of funds for everyday buyers. As a result, mortgage

lending is now at only fifty per cent of what it was in 2006 –
and worsening.

All this means that when times are hard, banks tighten their
belts and lend not only less overall but also less to any one
individual, even for very sound properties and where the
borrower has a good track record.

Deposits

It is still possible to borrow one hundred per cent of the
value of your home from a lender, but it is very hard. Most
lenders want at least a fifteen per cent deposit….and some
insist on much more. Some lenders are especially tough on
deposits for flats, and so on.

A deposit is the amount of your cash you are expected to put
down towards the value of your new home. Obviously, the
more you can afford, the less you'll have to borrow, and thus
pay interest on. But whilst this might at first appear
attractive, it could pay, in a rising property market, and
when interest rates are low, to borrow the most you can and
use your own money in other, more productive, ways. This
could, for example, mean keeping your own cash to run
your business, or to improve your property. You are then
effectively borrowing other people's money, based on the
value of your home, to do something else with the cash. This
cycle of cheap and readily-available money, based on the
value of private homes, is what has kept UK plc running a
break-neck speed from the mid 1990s until the current crash.

If you can put down a large proportion of the value of your
home from your own resources, the lender will feel more
comfortable and so lend you their cash at a lower interest
rate. They know that if the market takes a downturn their
money won't be at as great a risk as it would be were they

lending you the full one hundred per cent. After all, if the value of your home then falls it is you who'll take the first hit. Most first-time buyers traditionally put down between five and ten per cent in normal market conditions. Today this is rare, as lenders demand much more.

Affordability

Having decided how much cash you can cobble together to cover your deposit (and all the other expenses, see page 207) you'll next have to look at what level of debt you can afford to service. I use the word 'debt' advisedly as the whole of the mortgage industry would rather keep the word away from you. Make no mistake: what you are doing is getting into debt....for a huge amount of money.

An insurance company survey in mid-2008 found that nearly two million people said they couldn't afford to service their mortgage.

To a considerable extent the property market is driven by first-time buyers. Unless homes are affordable enough for them to climb onto the bottom rung of the ladder, others above them can't move up. Calculations by Citigroup, in August 2008, found that first-time buyers were spending more of their income on a home than at any time since 1974. With banks tightening up on loan-to-value ratios, the combined cost of a deposit and a first year's mortgage repayments came to sixty-nine per cent of the average first-time buyer's income.

Lenders should, of course, make affordability their main concern when offering large sums of money to people. For many years they have not been doing this. They are now being forced to do so in a big way as the credit crunch severely affects their *own* profits and even survival. The affordability issue is a very vexed one. It used to be said that mortgage servicing costs should never exceed one third of your total take-home pay, after tax. This makes servicing a mortgage pretty painless…and probably comparable with renting somewhere to live. However, as lenders got carried away with themselves over the last decade they've acted irresponsibly by offering borrowers amounts that require massive proportions of their take-home pay. This left borrowers open to personal financial crisis, or even repossession (see below) should their income fall or interest rates rise. Even those on fixed-rate mortgages (see below) cannot remain on them for ever and are in for a rude awakening once they start to pay at the current interest rate.

Something lenders seemed to have lost sight of is that most young couples can afford to service their debt only so long as both are employed. When one loses their job or the woman gets pregnant, income dramatically falls and they're in trouble. It makes sense not to borrow up to the hilt on both your salaries, however seductive this appears. I've been saying this to couples for years but until things take a downturn, as they have now, they haven't much cared to listen. This is understandable as people under about the age of forty have never experienced a property downturn and could hardly believe it would ever happen.

One way of making a deposit affordable and indeed the payments themselves more affordable, is to club together with a friend or even a group of friends to get a joint mortgage. This spreads the risk and makes buying possible when it might otherwise not be, even in todays market.

Self-certification (self-cert)
When you want to borrow money from a lender they'll ask for evidence of your income and outgoings. People who are

employed and on a salary are a good bet for lenders as there's nothing they like to see more than a regular payslip.

If you are self-employed, though, this can all be much trickier because although you may earn more than someone who is paid regularly by their boss, your income isn't assured, and lenders fear this insecurity.

Self-certified mortgages are those where you say what you expect to earn and the lender gives you what they think you can afford to service. Of course this opens itself to people bending the truth to exaggerate their earnings in order to secure a larger loan. For very obvious reasons, such individuals are at exceptional risk should there be a downturn in the economy or a serious hike in interest rates. This said, self-cert mortgages are still to be had, provided you can prove you have several sources of income. It also helps to have an experienced adviser.

How to pay the money back

Mortgage companies make their profits by charging you to borrow money at a higher interest rate than that for which they themselves can borrow it. But however much is borrowed, it'll have to be paid back.

There are several different ways of doing this and new 'products' are being dreamed up all the time. Whatever you pay, as briefly outlined below, there'll always be other costs, the largest of which is an Arrangement Fee. Such fees used to be so small that they didn't do much other than annoy. Today, though, when lenders are crazy for profit, as opposed to simply extending their market share, such fees have rocketed and can now amount to more than £2,000 for a large loan. Such large fees can be a serious deterrent to even very determined borrowers.

Another fee you may have to factor in is the Higher Lending Charge (HLC). This is a one-off insurance premium that some lenders charge borrowers who don't have much of a deposit. This fee can be added to your loan. Such an insurance benefits the lender should you default on your mortgage. You pay – they benefit! Wherever possible, try to avoid lenders who charge this fee.

Credit scoring

Before I look at the various types of mortgage, I must mention credit scoring. Many ordinary people are unaware that their total credit record is known and easily available...especially to anyone from whom they want to borrow money.

Every time you apply for credit of any kind you leave a 'footprint' on your file. The more footprints you have the more desperate it appears you are for credit. Obviously a potential lender will be concerned on seeing this. Such footprints remain on the file for six months. If you have county court judgements (CCJs) against you (a ruling in court that you cannot pay your debts), mortgage companies will not be keen to lend to you. These records stay on your files for seven years.

Strangely, if you have *never* had credit this too can go against you with a mortgage lender. At one extreme level, many years ago when living in the US, I had terrible problems because I had never borrowed anything from anyone there. I was a credit black hole! This was considered so unlikely that it sounded alarm bells....and created serious problems. What lenders want is to see that you can repay debt, be it on credit cards, rent, paying for a car, or servicing a mortgage. If you can't prove this, you could find it hard getting a mortgage, especially now.

There are credit reference agencies that keep records of all your credit transactions (even credit card applications that are refused). The main ones are Experian (www.experian.co.uk) and Equifax (www.checkmyfile.com). Before applying for a mortgage, go to one of these and check that your entry is correct. This will enable you to get mistakes altered before applying.

Lenders need to know whether or not someone has a poor credit history because although sub-prime mortgages (see page 58) account for only five per cent of the mortgage market, they contribute fifty per cent to the overall total of repossessions!

Types of mortgage

Repayment mortgages involve you agreeing a 'term' over which the money has to be repaid. This is usually twenty-five years but over recent times has gone to thirty, or even more, years. At one extreme, in the recent lending frenzy, some companies have given mortgages which are unlikely ever to be paid off in the borrower's lifetime! A 2008 study found that a quarter of home-owners are relying on an inheritance to pay off their mortgage!

Obviously, the longer the period over which you pay back the original capital, the lower the amount per month you'll pay today but the more interest you'll pay overall. With a repayment mortgage each month's payment contributes not only to paying off the actual loan amount but also to the interest you're building up. Early on, your monthly payments will consist almost entirely of interest but as the years go by you'll start paying off capital (the loan itself). Half-way through the life of your mortgage the balance of each month's payment will be fifty per cent capital and fifty per cent interest.

At the end of the agreed term you'll have paid off your debt. It's sobering to bear in mind that the total amount you'll have paid over the lifetime of the loan will be very much more than what you originally borrowed. This is a fact most of us choose to ignore when house prices are rising but if they are not it suddenly becomes a very unpleasant reality that you'll have paid far more for your home than it's worth. Such comparisons make renting look very attractive! Who said renting was money down the drain?

Interest-only mortgages are exactly what they say. You pay only interest to your lender. The amount you need to pay them off after the agreed term is produced by taking out some sort of savings vehicle that guarantees you'll have the cash to do so. Because these investment systems haven't done too well over recent years, it's vital to take professional advice if you're going this route. If you know you're going to come into money at some stage in the near-ish future you can just pay the interest and use your lump sum to pay off the loan capital. But paying off any borrowing earlier than you said you would, could cost you.

In the recent past there were three main 'investment vehicles' that people used to create a fund to pay off their mortgage. An endowment insurance policy; an ISA; or a pension of some kind. All have their pros and cons so be sure to take good advice before getting involved with any of them.

Early-repayment (redemption) penalties
Such penalties are common with many mortgage types, especially those that offer fixed interest rates.

Many mortgage types (see below) offer interest rate advantages provided you agree to be 'tied-in' to a certain length of time at this rate. The lender then borrows this cash and lends it to you on the basis that they'll make a profit on borrowing it for the time you both agreed. If you choose to repay earlier, it'll cost them lost income. They seek to make up for this loss by charging you an early-repayment penalty. This can come to many thousands of pounds. A tiered-penalty system is one where the amount you pay to redeem the loan early reduces as the years go by.

Should you want to transfer your mortgage from one home to another with the same lender you can usually do so without paying this type of early redemption penalty.

Mortgage types at a glance

All the types I describe here were available just before I started writing the book. As 2008 has passed, many products have been withdrawn from the market, leaving a much smaller selection of possibilities. By the time this book is in bookshops, I have no doubt that the picture will have changed yet again. When conditions are rosy, lenders are in the business to gain and maintain market share. In these happy times they create products that give early advantages to borrowers and seduce them to come to them rather go to someone else. When the going gets tough, and there's not that much cash to lend to anyone, all this disappears and people get desperate to find a mortgage at all.

Variable-rate: Here the interest rate you pay varies and tracks the Bank of England's monthly base-rate and London Interbank Lending Rate (LIBOR). Unfortunately, as many have found to their horror recently, rate reductions may not be passed on to borrowers – either in full, or at all – when lenders find themselves in financial difficulty or just want to save for their future. Increases in interest rates are, in contrast, usually passed on very quickly.

Fixed-rate: Here, you set the rate at which you will pay, and you pay this for an agreed length of time and at an increased rate. This gives you the ability to plan your outgoings as they'll be the same every month for the term agreed. You'll be tied in for the duration of the term for which you've fixed, and even possibly for longer. Once your fixed-interest term is up, your mortgage will revert to a higher variable rate, leaving you at the mercy of the market. Having become used to an artificially-low interest rate things can get tricky if you have to pay a lot more per month. Going the fixed-rate route will usually cost you to get out of (see early repayment penalties, above).

Discount: This is a variable-rate mortgage but with a discount on the normal rate. You are tied into the mortgage at this discounted rate for the term agreed and even possibly beyond.

Capped-rate: Here your interest rate will be capped to a maximum that cannot be exceeded. If your lender's variable rate goes above this your rate will be capped but when rates fall you benefit. Once more you'll be tied in for a fixed period. This type is hardly available now.

Cashback: This type of mortgage is a 'bribe' to get your business. You may get cash in the here-and-now or on completion of the loan. This type is not available now.

Flexible: This type suits a lot of people as it allows them to under- or over-pay as their circumstances change. You can also borrow money from your loan free of charge. There are no tie-ins with flexible loans. Such mortgages calculate your interest on a daily basis, depending on the amount you are borrowing at that moment. This system can work well if you think you're going to come into some cash and will want to pay off a chunk of your mortgage. These mortgages are usually provided at variable rates of interest.

Offset: This is just like a flexible mortgage but brings your savings into the pot too. Because you pay less interest (your savings reduce the total debt) your repayment period is shorter and the mortgage thus cheaper over its lifetime. Talk to your IFA about the balance of savings to loan and how this suits your circumstances best. Interest rates for offset mortgages are higher than average and really only make sense if you have a large amount saved.

Current account: This is a bit like an offset mortgage but here all your balances go into one financial pot. All your debt, including that on credit cards, is now charged at the cheaper mortgage rate and your income goes straight into the pot, thus reducing the debt.

Base-rate tracker: Here your interest rate is linked to the Bank of England base rate but any reductions in rate are passed on in full, unlike with some variable-rate products. A margin is set and the lender has to stick to it. These mortgages are still popular, even in today's difficult economic climate.

Some lending institutions will provide you with a certificate that says a loan will be made available to you, provided the property is OK'd by their surveyor. In this market it's vital to have some sort of commitment from a lender before even going out into the marketplace to look for your new home. There are masses of properties for sale out there but not many people with cash in their pocket. Your whole credibility and value to a vendor will be greatly enhanced if you have your loan sorted out well before you go to see their home. If you are a cash buyer this is even better.

As I write this, lenders are being very cautious with their money and are not, as they used to, lending it to their competitors. This, coupled with various unsettling financial crises in the US, has made everyone in the money-lending world wary and, as a result, it is very hard to obtain a mortgage at all. This will all settle down eventually, but no-one can say when. In my opinion, it could take a few years.

Falling behind with your mortgage payments

The key thing here is to be straight with yourself as soon as you realise you've got a problem. Don't go into denial, or 'helpless and hopeless' mode. Many people leave things so long, their debt gets out of hand. Acting quickly and early reduces your chances of being repossessed. Get a friend or caring person to help you, or go to an advice bureau.

The first step is to talk to your lender. They'll want to help because they don't want repossessed homes on their books! Go to them with a plan as to how you'll manage your way out of the situation. Understandably, they'll want to see what you're earning, how you intend to earn more (or borrow from a private source, perhaps), and how they could help make your life easier. You might be able to freeze repayments for a while; have an interest holiday; take out a different type of mortgage; reduce or even temporarily stop the payments on an endowment policy; surrender your endowment policy and take the money; or extend the period of your loan so as to make repayments cheaper in the here-and-now. Never forget, they make money out of lending you money so they'll try to find a way of keeping you in debt…as long as you can service it somehow. Unfortunately, lending institutions that have accepted public money to keep afloat are anxious to show what good custodians they are of their new funds by being tough on defaulting borrowers. However, this places them in a difficult, somewhat 'schizophrenic' position, because coupled with this desire to be seen not to waste public money, they also need to maintain a human face after the taxpayer has bailed them out.

It will greatly help in all this if you discuss things with an adviser before talking to your lender. This could be an accountant, a mortgage broker or a citizen's advice centre, or you could call the National Debtline 0808 808 4000 or go to www.nationaldebtline.co.uk. All of these will tell you that you should make paying your mortgage your first priority. The last thing you'll want is to lose your home. Talking of which, never hand your keys back to your lender without taking professional advice first. This seemingly easy way out of your dilemma could land you in more problems.

But whatever solution you come up with you'll almost definitely need to change your way of life so you can afford your repayments. This is likely to mean spending less; cutting out non-essentials; reducing your insurance costs if you can; and taking a hard, honest look at how you live.

Re-mortgaging
Finally, it can be tempting to consolidate all your debts and take out a new, larger mortgage on more acceptable terms. At the moment, the only game in town for mortgage lenders is re-mortgaging. Attractive though this is, be very careful because your financial status might not change in the way you hope and you could be stuck with an even bigger debt, perhaps for a lot longer. With unemployment set to rise and prices of essentials going up by the week, it might not be a great time to saddle yourself with more debt. You could also be in trouble with under-valuing (see page 109). Take good professional advice before doing anything.

Insurance

People differ a lot in their attitude to insurance. Some would never move a muscle without it and others think it's a waste of money. When finances are tight it's tempting to skimp on insurance. But this is very unwise.

There are several different types of insurance you'll need to think about:

Buildings insurance

This is compulsory if you are borrowing money to pay for your home. It covers the building itself and all the fixtures (kitchens, bathrooms etc), should your home be flooded, catch fire, or have a tree fall on it, for example. The policy covers you for all your costs right up to, and including, having the whole place rebuilt from scratch. It's vital to keep this policy up to date for the correct amount or you might find that if you want to claim, the insurance company will pay only a fraction of what things actually cost as you'll be under-insured. This can be extremely costly. The insurance valuation bears no relationship to the market value of your home – it is based on what it would cost to rebuild it.

Home contents insurance

Well worth having in case you are burgled, or your belongings are destroyed by fire or flood. Even if you think you'll never be flooded (there are no waterways close by), just remember this could easily happen if someone were to leave the bath overflowing. The damage this can cause is terrible. A new-for-old policy is best because if your TV is stolen you won't want a five-year-old model as a replacement! With a 'cash' policy, your insurer gives you money and you go out and get the replacement item.

Mortgage repayment insurance

Contrary to what many people believe, the Government has no duty to pay your mortgage if you cannot do so for some reason – usually because you've lost your job. Mortgage Payment Protection Insurance enables you to agree in advance on a time delay (30, 60 or 90 days, or even longer), after which the policy will kick in and pay your monthly repayments so you don't lose your home. There are many variations on this theme.

Life assurance

Such policies enable you to pay off your mortgage if you die before you've paid it back. These policies are usually based on some sort of life cover. Should you die, the mortgage is paid off and your family can stay in their home. There are several variations on this type of insurance.

Critical illness cover

Look carefully at what illnesses are covered before you decide on this one. If you become seriously ill and can't work, your monthly repayments will be met.

As there's so much money to be made from insuring for such risks there are many providers offering their products. A good IFA, mortgage broker, insurance broker, or even your lender, will be able to advise you. Simple home contents policies can even be obtained from certain supermarkets! The internet is also a good place to look around and price comparison sites can be very useful.

How to find a property

Estate agents

The overwhelming majority of home buyers use an estate agent. Even if you start by looking on line you'll invariably end up with an agent. They'll be especially keen to sell you a new home when they have lots of stock and will tend to be highly realistic about the price of both what you are selling and what you are proposing to buy. They should know – especially in current market conditions – which sellers are motivated to sell and will help you save time by viewing only those properties where the vendors are realistic about their asking price. A good local agent will also be aware of distressed sellers, be they private or commercial, and could put you in the way of a bargain.

Choosing an agent. The best way of choosing an agent is to ask friends who they've found to be helpful. Look also at my guidelines about agents on page 112.

When you register with agents, be straight about what you can afford to pay, and make sure you've done your homework in advance so you can tell the agent exactly what you're looking for. A good agent will not just listen to what you say but will also read between the lines and offer you things that you might not have otherwise thought of. It's very unusual for people to end up buying exactly what they thought they would in terms of price or property.

Although agents act for sellers, it's vital to get any agent you're dealing with on your side. Try to make an ally of them and they'll pull out the stops for you. We all like to be liked and to feel valued, so be fair, straight, flexible and reliable and you'll find most agents will go that extra mile.

It's best to choose agents who are members of one of the professional organisations, because you'll probably get a better service and will certainly be able to take action should things go wrong. There are two main representative bodies: The Royal Institution of Chartered Surveyors (www.rics.org) and the National Association of Estate Agents (www.naea.co.uk). The Ombudsman for Estate Agents (www.oea.co.uk) regulates the activities of agents, whether they are members of the RICS or the NAEA, or not.

These bodies will help if you need to complain about any aspect of the service you receive from an affiliated body. Bear in mind, though, that fewer agents are members of the RICS than of the NAEA. However, the rule of the RICS are much stricter and penalties higher in the event of negligence. The NAEA is a trade body set up by its members to look after *their* interests, whereas the RICS also enjoys a public-interest role by virtue of its royal charter. This means there's a greater responsibility on its members to deliver.

Property ads in the papers

Always a favourite. Almost all of these will be in the hands of agents but it's often possible to discover good agents this way, and possibly ones you didn't even know existed from looking on your high street. There'll also be a few private sellers who can be worth following up. If you're buying in an unfamiliar area, get the local papers sent to you for a few weeks. This not only puts you into touch with the local agents (which, in fairness, you could do on the internet) but it'll help you decide whether the area is your sort of place. Local papers are a fund of valuable insights.

The internet

Now a massive player. All good agents have their own websites and if you are new to an area, simply entering 'sale property XXtown' will get you started within minutes. There are several good 'facilitator' sites, too, such as:

- Rightmove.co.uk
- FindaProperty.com
- Fish4homes.co.uk
- Primelocation.co.uk
- Vebra.com
- Hotproperty.co.uk

These all have a part to play, although sometimes you'll find that properties which have been sold stay on longer than they should, and new instructions can take a while to be displayed. There is probably no better alternative than a mutually-responsive relationship with local agents who are likely to offer the sort of property you're looking for. Make sure they know about changes in your circumstances.

Keeping your eyes peeled

Agents' boards; new sites developers are about to build on, or which are already under construction; auction notices; and so on can all get you started.

Word of mouth can be important too. For example, if you're looking for a flat in a particular block or development, speak to the porter, or chairman of the residents' association. I have, on several occasions, found this produced a result.

On page 202 I list all the questions a seller needs to be able to answer when showing their home. Go to this list and check out all the items that you'll need to be sure of before you decide on a property.

Legal types of property

Freehold

Here, you own not just the house or flat but also the land on which it sits. This means you don't pay anyone ground rent or service charges and that you have much more control over what you can do to both house and land. This type of 'tenure' (as it's known), is the best to have but bear in mind that you may still be subject to certain restrictions as far as decoration or extension if the property is on a development old or new – or in a Conservation Area.

Leasehold

In this, you own the property for the duration of the lease but not the land on which it sits. The person who owns the land is called the freeholder. He will charge you ground rent every year. The length of a lease on the land is very important when buying. A new-build may have a lease of 999 years, which means that it is effectively like owning the freehold. Leases shorter than about fifty years are a problem for many lenders, especially when times are tight, because they could see themselves being left with a property, the value of which is falling year on year. Generally speaking, once a lease length falls to below about fifty years, the value of the building on it reduces every year to take into account that the property will eventually become the owner's again. There are ways of extending a lease and groups of leaseholders (such as in a block of flats) can get together and buy the freehold from the freeholder and take over its management. Such individuals then each own a property that has a 'share of the freehold'.

Virtually every flat in England and Wales is owned on a long leasehold basis for a fixed term of years. Under Part 1 of the

Leasehold Reform, Housing and Urban development Act 1993, as well as the Commonhold and Leasehold Reform Act of 2002, leaseholders enjoy the right – subject to certain criteria – to collectively purchase the freehold in their building, or to extend their lease by a further 90 years at no ground rent for the remainder of the term. The buying of the freehold can be complicated and can involve negotiations with the other lessees, the freeholder and his representatives. If you want to cut down on the amount of stress involved in all this, get a surveyor who has the necessary experience, to act on your behalf, without having to refer the matter to the Leasehold Valuation Tribunal, if at all possible. This latter route is even more costly and time consuming.

A useful source of help on leaseholds is www.lease-advice.org.uk

Making an offer

Once you've chosen the place you think you want, it's time to make an offer. When there's lots of choice, as there is in this market, you may decide to make an offer that's well below the asking price, depending on your judgement, and that of the agent. It's in your best interests to look out for that committed seller who really wants, or has, to sell. There's no point wasting your time with people who are not absolutely motivated to sell. In a seller's market you have to deal with such people but now you're in the driving seat, you do not. Agents too, are adopting the same principle.

It is usual for the buyer to tell the seller's agent what they want to offer for the property and for the agent to relay this offer to the vendor. Although you might want to make this offer yourself, I advise you keep out of it. The agent is paid to do the best for his client (the vendor) but he'll be very realistic indeed at the moment and will want to get a sale from his own point of view as much as the vendor's. He has his overheads to pay and may, as times are so hard, have already laid off staff and cut back in various other ways. This will mean he'll encourage vendors to be sensible about their response to your offer or they could be left waiting for another (possibly lower one) for many months. 'A bird in the hand' is the motto in a buyers' market. If you make a very low offer, which the seller dismisses out of hand, when you increase your bid, the owner may not take you, or your offer, very seriously.

When making an offer it'll help if you provide some of your thinking to the agent. For example you could say; 'The place needs totally redecorating throughout and I noticed all the fences were down. The heating is many years old and will cost several thousand to put right. Because of this I'd like to offer X'. You can make your offer as cheeky as you feel you can get away with in a buyer's market but very few people will be prepared to take extremely low offers unless they are selling in distress.

If you are really interested in a property, I think it's a good idea to develop a relationship with the vendor. Keep your agent informed but this good relationship will help build trust between the parties so that if anything goes wrong they're more likely to understand and perhaps even extend a deadline for exchange of contracts.

Over perhaps two or three offers and some to-ing and fro-ing by the agent you'll probably come to an agreed price. You now make your offer 'subject to contract'. In other words, you are not bound to buy until you actually have a signed contract between you, and this could take some weeks. In Scotland, the system is that once an offer has been accepted there's a deal; the price cannot be altered and you're bound to buy.

On acceptance of your offer

Appoint a solicitor or licensed conveyancer
They'll then get cracking on the legal side. You may be required to put down some sort of 'holding deposit'. This is usually a small sum of, say, £500 or £1,000. It shows you are serious but doesn't bind you to buying. On exchange of contracts (see below) you'll generally have to come up with a deposit of five to ten per cent of the agreed purchase price. If you are also selling somewhere you might be able to arrange for the deposit you're receiving from your buyer to be put aside to pay for the deposit on your purchase. Talk to your legal professional.

If you can't lay your hands on the ten per cent, you might be able to use a 'deposit guarantee scheme'. Your legal adviser will organise this with an insurance company. You could also borrow the money, or raise it in any way you choose. It pays to start thinking about how you'll finance the deposit as soon as you think about buying somewhere. To find a licensed conveyancer, go to www.theclc.gov.uk

To find a solicitor who will do this sort of work, ask the selling agent, get recommendations from friends, and if this doesn't produce a result, go to www.lawsociety.org.uk

Whoever you intend to use, first ask them how much they'll charge. There used to be a fixed scale of charges for such work but there aren't any more. Be sure to ask:

- Whether the fee they quote will be fixed, or depend on how much work they end up doing
- Whether this fee covers all the other outgoings such as office expenses (photocopying etc); land registration fees; local authority search fees; and Stamp Duty
- How they'll charge should things get complicated and take a lot more time than they'd planned for
- What'll happen fees-wise if the sale falls through

If you are buying the property with another person, your solicitor or conveyancer will advise you on matters such as joint ownership and beneficial ownership. The latter comes in two forms. If you are 'joint tenants' you both own the place but you must both agree to its being sold. If one of you dies, that share goes to the other as of right. If you are 'tenants in common', you'll each have a share in the property that you can sell if you want. These shares don't necessarily have to be equal. When you die your share can go to whomever you decide.

Talk to your lender

The lender will want to have the place valued. At the moment lenders are being very very cautious about value and some are seriously under-valuing the properties they're being asked to lend on, on the basis that prices could fall yet further and they'd be left with a deficit if they had to repossess them. Some valuers are reducing values dramatically, so don't be surprised if what you've agreed to pay and what the lender says they think it's worth is rather different. The problem here is not simply academic, of course. Your lender will take their valuer's suggestion as the basis for what they'll lend on. If he reduces the value by, say, twenty-five per cent, then this will be their 'one hundred per cent' for the purposes of your borrowing. If you want and can get, only a seventy-five per cent mortgage, this will seventy-five per cent of *their* definition of one hundred per cent, not yours. This is just one of the very difficult features of the current property market.

This valuation will be carried out on behalf of your lender, though you'll pay for it! It is not a survey for you and tells you nothing at all about any problems with the place. For this you'll need to have your own survey done.

Get the place surveyed

Although a substantial proportion of people in normal markets don't bother to do this I think they're mad unless the place is new or so nearly new that it is covered by some sort of builder's warranty (such as NHBC). This surveyor will now act on your behalf to tell you what he thinks the place is worth and what, if anything, needs doing to it. There are two basic types of house survey:

Building survey. Here, the surveyor produces a detailed report involving several hours of carefully assessing and photographing all the structures of the house, some of which may be hidden. He'll look at the roof and the chimneys; whether the walls are straight and vertical; assess the foundation type; how the walls are made; see how the drains work; assess the house's insulation levels; what changes have been made and whether the correct permission has been obtained for them; the general condition of the place; whether there are any issues that could prove expensive in the future (subsidence or major defects anywhere); checking there's no damp anywhere; whether there's evidence of rot or worm in structural timbers; and much more. The report will run into many pages and will tell you in detail what's good and what's bad about the place. He may then be able to give you an idea of how much any such work will cost to carry out. You, in turn, could now go back to the vendor's agent and tell him you want the price adjusted accordingly. Or, if things are really worrying, you might decide to abort entirely and start again with another, less troublesome, property.

Obviously, this sort of survey is vital with older properties, listed homes and larger places. It's also important if there's anything unusual about the property, such as it currently being flats and you want to make it into a single home again. If in any doubt, ask a surveyor what he thinks a lender will need in your situation. Their own surveyor will have his own views, of course!

Homebuyer survey and valuation. This is a much lower-key affair that involves reporting only on those things that can be readily seen. It usually concentrates on those aspects of the structure which require more urgent or significant attention and which might compromise its current and future re-sale value. The surveyor might suggest specialists get involved (for example for rot or woodworm).

Clearly, such a survey costs a lot less. But then it can pick up only very obvious matters and you could be buying a lot of trouble, especially in an older or unusual house.

There's a lot more information about surveys on www.rics.org/Property/ResidentialProperty

Negotiating and completing your purchase

Your legal professional will do all the necessary work involved in drawing up a contract which will be signed by both the seller and yourself. On the lodging of a deposit, this becomes a legally-binding document. This 'exchange of contracts', as it is known, is the critical day in your buying journey because from then on you have to go ahead with the purchase and you'll need to get the property insured as you'll be its legal owner.

In order to produce a contract for you to sign, your legal adviser will look into everything that might affect the property (technically called 'making enquiries and searches'), so you can relax knowing that there won't suddenly be an airport next to you in two years, for example. You'll also be made aware of material issues that affect the property such as boundaries, disputes with neighbours, what exactly is included in the sale apart from just the house itself, and so on. There is a standard form that the seller has to complete giving much of this information. Enquiries also have to made of the Land Registry, to be sure that the piece of land on which your proposed home sits actually belongs to the people selling it. It's now that you'll discover that the neighbours have been using a part of your garden to park their caravan, thinking the land was theirs!

This is also the time to look again at what your surveyor has reported and what your response is to his findings. Your adviser will take you through all this and will also be talking to the lender you intend to use to be sure the mortgage is set up as it should be. Your lender may have views on what their surveyor discovered, especially in a tough market, when they're likely to be much more picky than normal.

On signing this contract and handing over an agreed deposit (usually five or ten per cent of the sale price) the contract is binding on both parties. You now have to buy at that price in an agreed timescale and the vendor must sell to you on this basis.

After a period (usually about a month after exchange of contracts, but it can be as short as a day, if you so arrange it) you'll 'complete' on the sale and the house will be yours to move in to. Before this happens your lender will have to have released the money; the deeds of the house will be given to your legal adviser by the seller's solicitor; and the seller will hand over the keys so you can formally gain access to the property. Most people move into their new home on completion day but this isn't necessary.

If at any stage there's anything that concerns you, talk to your legal adviser. No one will have a more intense interest in the subject than you, so it pays to keep a close personal eye on everything almost every day.

Buying a home at auction

In troubled times it can make especially good sense to buy a property at auction. Lenders usually off-load their repossessions at auctions but in addition to properties that have been foreclosed on, there are other opportunities out there for the canny buyer. When the market softens, all kinds of property slowly emerges from the shadows...sometimes very interesting propositions that made financial sense to the owner at one stage but are now impossible to develop – for one of many reasons.

Buying at auction has the advantage of being quite quick and produces a definite result on the day. There's no gazumping or game-playing. Another advantage is that you'll be dealing direct with the competition. This should mean what you'll pay will be a fair market price. The downside is that once you hear the gavel go down, you're committed! No second thoughts are possible. If you *do* have a change of heart, it'll cost you dearly.

Choosing your auctioneer

Once you begin to think about buying at auction, start going to local sales to see how they work. Decide exactly what type of property you want to buy and then look at the ads in the papers; subscribe to some auction mailing lists (on paper or on-line); take out a subscription to the *Estates Gazette*; subscribe to *Property Auction News*; look in *Property Week*; look on the internet for auction houses that deal with your kind of property; and go around your desired area looking for auction boards. Auctioneers' catalogues are usually printed two or three weeks before the sale. They are also available on-line. Details of forthcoming auctions can be found on the auctioneers' websites too.

Appointing your team

Buying at auction isn't easy. Remember...the day you buy is the day you make your profit! But it's easy to make mistakes and lose money. TV shows never make this clear, but then it wouldn't make great telly! If you're a seasoned pro who is used to buying at auction you'll already have a good team around you but if you're using the downturn in prices to get into property developing, or even to find a new home for yourself, you'll need all the help you can get. You'll be up against three main groups of pros: entrepreneurs, builders, and investors.

Entrepreneurs are opportunists who are simply looking for places to invest their cash and get a good return. Such people may not be all that interested in property but see low values as a time to invest and sell on later, at the right time. Builders are looking for opportunities to keep their men employed and to make money, though not necessarily huge amounts of money in a recession.

Lastly are the investors who'll be looking to increase their property portfolio, taking a long-term view. This latter group will have long since re-mortgaged on the back of their existing property portfolio (when mortgages were available) and are now in cash, sitting around waiting for the property market to bottom out. They will then leap back in.

You, however, may be a home-owner searching for a bargain-priced place to live, perhaps to move down-market, or even having been repossessed.

The business of buying a property at auction starts many weeks before the actual sale day. People you'll need in your team include:

An accountant. You'll need financial advice at every stage. Someone who knows your whole financial picture can tell you the ins and outs of the tax implications of what you're planning. It's vital in a bad market not to make mistakes. Good advice is all the more important if you intend to buy the property through a private company or a trust; make the property part of your pension fund; or buy through an overseas vehicle.

A solicitor. He or she will be an invaluable team member in troubled markets because some of the properties being offered at auction could have legal or other negative histories that could fool even very professional investors. You have only to make one small mistake over a tenancy agreement or a boundary, for example, to find your plans going pear-shaped in a moment.

A builder. I think a 'tame' builder is one of the best allies to have. As you'll see from the timetable below, you'll need someone on tap who can quickly and accurately price the building work that needs doing on your candidate property. Someone you know and trust, and who has preferably worked for you before, is ideal. When times are tough there are very good builders all too willing to help in this way. A local builder will have insights into what similar houses have needed doing (and at what cost); will know the local planners and what they'll allow; and will have other professionals he can draw upon, should you need them.

A surveyor. This professional's advice could be a deal-breaker. It's impossible for you to assess how serious a bad wall, a large crack, or a bowed roof is without the help of a structural surveyor. On the one hand something can look terrible and put other buyers off when, in reality, there's nothing much wrong. On the other, a small defect can be the symptom of a much deeper 'disease' and should warn off all but the most professional developers, or those with deep pockets!

A *helpful partner or friend*. We all need someone who can help us stand back from a project and take an outsider's view. Many of us get carried away with enthusiasm when we see something we fancy – especially if it seems a bargain – but buying at auction isn't about emotion; it's a hard-nosed business. You'll be up against far more experienced and richer people than yourself, so be wary of apparent bargains and listen to those who care about you.

Money matters

Even before you start looking for a property, decide what you can afford. Rest assured that you'll kiss many a frog before you get that prince, so don't be disappointed if you don't get the first property you set your heart on. Buying at auction is a process rather than a goal. Simply having the cash might not be enough.

This said, it's vital to get your cash sorted out well in advance of an auction. The auction house will want cleared funds on the day. Remember that the purchase price of a property is only one of the expenses at this stage. You may, for example, in addition to your deposit, have to pay the vendor's local search fees and legal conveyancing charges; the auctioneer's administrative charges; and local authority surveyor's charges. This could all tot up to a few thousand pounds. Check all the expenses with the auctioneer well in advance of the sale. For more on buying costs see page 207.

When paying on the day, auction houses will accept any form of cleared funds. It's best not to try to pay with cash as things are now so tight on money-laundering. You can pay by a banker's draft, or a cheque. Debit cards are now accepted by many auction houses. When arranging for cleared funds, allow yourself a little leeway above the ten per cent deposit value in case you get over-enthusiastic on the day! Be sure to have at least one legally-recognised form of identification to take with you to the sale as you will need to prove your identity to comply with the Money Laundering Regulations 2003. Your funds will be kept safely in the bank account of the auction house and they will earn and retain the interest on it for the month pending completion of the sale.

If you are intending to bid by phone, internet, fax or letter (known as bidding by proxy) you'll need to lodge the deposit money with the auctioneer several days in advance of the sale.

Assessing value

Once you've decided on a target property, try to asses its value by:

Looking in local estate agents to see what similar things are going for. The vital thing here is not to be fooled by asking prices in a falling market. You are only interested in what properties actually *sell* for. Look on the Land Registry website (www.uk-landregistry.co.uk) to see what houses in your street, or area, have actually achieved. Local estate agents or a local surveyor will be helpful too. The thing with auctions is that you can never know the motives of other bidders in the room on the day. This means that you must decide on your maximum price before you go to the sale, and then stick to it. If a rival bidder has lived next door for years and has been waiting for the place to come up for his mother, he'll outbid you every time. Remember, too, that the day you buy is the day you sell.

Things to think about when valuing a property include:

- **The condition:** if in any doubt, get professional advice from a builder or surveyor. Many properties offered at auction are in poor condition, which is why they can be a bargain. Of course, not all bad-condition properties actually are bargains, so you'll need to take advice. In difficult financial times people will also have let the upkeep of their properties go, either because they know they'll lose them back to their lender; because they just haven't got the cash to look after them whatever they'd like to do; and even, in some cases, because they are so angry about being repossessed that they actually trash the place

- **How much needs to be done to bring it up to standard:** an estate agent will guide you as to what's needed to make the place commercially viable

- **What comparable homes have sold for recently** (not more than three months ago)

- **What could be done to it to increase its value**…and at what cost (for example, making more bedrooms, converting a loft, or creating parking space). Again, a local agent or surveyor will advise you

- **How its use could be changed to make it more valuable** – changing a shop or a disused dairy into a home, for example. Talk to a designer, or even the local planning department

- **What's happening to the area**. Buying in a currently unfashionable but up-and-coming area is a good bet. Look for skips in surrounding roads; find out about proposed transport improvements; ask the council about any proposed leisure facilities and new schools. Keep your eyes open for new pubs, coffee shops, restaurants, etc. Look out for evidence of new shopping facilities. See what the big developers are up to (if they're busy locally you can be sure they've done their homework and could be worth following). Buy the local papers for several weeks to get a feel for the local politics and issues

The guide price and the reserve price

The guide price is the amount the vendor would like for the property. Close to the auction day they'll talk to the auctioneer who'll advise them whether the reserve price (see below) should be higher or lower than this. His decision will be based on many things, including the level of interest shown by viewers.

The reserve price is that below which the vendor (and thus the auctioneer) will not sell. It is usually fairly close to the guide price and is the vital figure at any auction. Rather obviously, auctioneers don't usually let this sum out beforehand! Some public bodies, when selling off property, give the auctioneer a sealed envelope which he is allowed to open only as he mounts the rostrum. The exception to the reserve price secrecy rule is when a property is cheap and a sale vital. Here the auction house may publish a reserve in the catalogue to drum up interest and get bums on seats. Usually, though, the reserve price secrecy greatly helps the auctioneer to play the room in a way that sells the lot at the best possible price. This, after all, is his job as he is acting for the seller, not you.

Part of the reserve price game on the day is for the auctioneer to use all his wiles, acting abilities and experience not to divulge when the reserve is reached. If you fancy yourself at body language, however, you could try out your skills to good effect. By being there from the very start of the auction you'll be able to watch carefully how the auctioneer behaves when a lot is sold, and when one is not sold. This could help you when it comes to your lot. In a busy professional sale room twenty or more lots could go under the hammer every hour so you should have plenty of opportunity to wise up on the auctioneer's style.

It can be very handy to know what lots actually sell for at auction. A good website is that of The Essential Information Group (tel: 0870 112 3040). Some auction houses regularly publish lists of results soon after a sale.

The dress rehearsal

Seasoned auctioneers suggest that novices do a complete dummy run with an actual property they might, in theory, want but aren't actually going to buy. Look at the timetable below and go through the stages with your 'fantasy property'. You'll be astonished at what confidence this can give you, if you're new to the game. Buying at auction is always a bit nerve-wracking but this real-life rehearsal will give you a head-start.

The run-up to an auction

Most auctioneers start to market properties about a month before the actual sale day.

Once you've identified your candidate property (or properties) this is the start of your race to the finishing line. Every day from now on will cost you time, effort, and money as you do your careful homework. At any stage you must be strong enough to back out if you don't like the 'feel' of the property as you learn more about it. This can be hard for novices who fall for something and take a lot of convincing that it isn't right. Pros never do this. They know very well that properties are like London buses...there's always another one around the corner!

Tasks you need to achieve, in this order, include:

As soon as you possibly can and definitely within ten days:
- Do your first inspection (see above)
- Check the auctioneer's details against what's actually at the property
- Obtain a legal pack: copies can be obtained by mail or e-mail
- Get the place independently valued by a surveyor or a local estate agent
- Carefully go through the auction house's Conditions of Sale. These can be numerous and very detailed. If in any doubt, ask an advice centre or a solicitor to explain things
- If the place looks a runner, see your accountant, solicitor and finance source. Ask your solicitor to start the ball rolling with the vendor's solicitor
- Talk to your lender. Many auction houses have details of those willing to lend on properties bought at auction

Over the next ten days:
- Go to the property again, this time being really critical. Take someone with you for a second opinion, and your builder to price any work that needs doing
- Consider making an offer before the auction. This is what many pros do. They try to avoid the competition of the sale room at all costs. This is, however, a bit of a gamble because the auctioneer cannot 'un-know' what he knows. He and the seller can now adjust the reserve

price because they know you will go at least that far. You have declared your position, which can weaken your hand on the day. If you badly want a property, a pre-auction offer can be a good route to go but you might just over-pay. But then buying at auction is for those with a gambling spirit! If you intend to go this pre-auction route be prepared to exchange contracts very quickly indeed

In the final week:
- Decide how much you're going to bid
- Arrange your finances and have cleared funds ready
- Get your solicitor along for the sale, if you want him there
- If you can't get to the auction you can bid by proxy (your solicitor, or other professional, can bid for you or you can bid remotely by phone, fax, or on the internet). Talk to the auction house about this well in advance of sale day
- Attend the auction if you possibly can

On the day
- Get there in plenty of time. Check that there aren't any changes to the details of your property. All manner of things can come to light between the printing of the official catalogue and sale day. And there may be typographical and other human errors in the catalogue. At worst, the lot you wanted could have been withdrawn, or even sold, prior to the auction
- Register
- Listen carefully to the auctioneer's opening speech not only is it usually interesting but it could contain information about your lot. It will certainly inform you of the way his auction house works and what to do, should you be successful in your bid

- Make your first bid very clear to be certain you're not overlooked. Many auctioneers have 'spotters' alongside them to be sure that bids aren't missed. These are especially useful at larger sales where there could be two hundred or so people in the room. Interestingly, only about ten per cent of all those attending an auction are there to bid. Bear in mind that the auctioneer may be bidding on behalf of the seller and could thus be taking bids 'off the wall, or 'off the chandelier'. If you are really keen to get the lot, try a 'jump bid'. Here you leap way above what everyone else is offering. This can put you in a strong psychological position as other bidders perceive you to be determined to outbid them whatever they offer, and so back off
- The auctioneer's aim is to pace the bidding in large increments at a time. In this way he tempts bidders to rush on and 'over-spend', thus getting the best price for his client. Professional auction buyers, on the other hand, want to slow down this gallop by offering small increases. By forcing the auctioneer to take smaller increments early you'll make your opposition bid time and again, leading them to believe you're stretching yourself to your limits when in fact you'll come in with a final bid and clinch the deal
- As long as you are interested in a particular lot, keep eye contact with the auctioneer. Once you've reached your limit, stop whatever you were doing to attract his attention and look away
- Never bid more than the amount you agreed with yourself beforehand. The moment the gavel hits the table, a legal contract is created. Your signing of the piece of paper afterwards is purely a formality. This law is what makes purchasing at auction so different from other types of buying
- Complete a purchase slip and go to the contracts desk

- Sign the contract or memorandum before leaving
- Give your solicitor's details
- Pay your purchaser's administration fee
- Pay your deposit

If the property is unsold, go to the auctioneer immediately afterwards and express your interest. The vendor may be so disappointed at not getting a sale that a deal could be done. Many a good bargain can be picked up on these so-called 'withdrawn' lots. At this stage the auctioneer may come clean about the reserve price. After all, he really wants a sale. If you can't do a deal on the day, talk to the auction house a week later to see what's happened.

Immediately after the sale day

If you thought your work was done on leaving the sale room, you'd be wrong.

Things to do now include:
- Getting the contract (signed by you and the vendor) to your solicitor for his immediate action. You have only 20 working days to get everything done and dusted. This time flies by, so don't sit around
- Insuring the property. The minute the gavel falls, it's your responsibility to have insurance cover for the structure
- Getting the place secured if it is empty, or likely to be subject to vandalism or break-in. Change all the locks, anyway
- Informing your lender that you have bought the property
- Going through your finances again with your accountant
- Doing everything your solicitor needs to ensure completion

- Arranging the funds to complete the deal. You'll have, thus far, paid only the 10% deposit
- Getting quotes for any urgent work that needs doing
- Completing on the sale. If you don't complete within the agreed and contracted time-scale (usually twenty working days from the auction), the seller can legally keep your deposit and re-sell the house. If it sells for less than you agreed to pay he can come to you for the difference (plus any expenses and costs). This is obviously not a route you'll want to take.

Chapter 9
REPOSSESSION

When a lender provides money for you to buy your home they do so on the express understanding that they can get their cash back if you cannot keep up the payments you agreed to make. When such a lender takes action to get their money back they can 'repossess' your home. This means they take it from you and sell it to recoup their money.

Although it might appear that these companies are big bad wolves, in fact they really don't want your home at all….they're in the business of making money out of 'renting out' money….not in the property business. Large portfolios of repossessed homes are, in fact, a nuisance and embarrassment to lenders. This is one reason they'll fall over themselves to help you keep your home, if at all possible.

This said, there's a group of less-than-scrupulous outfits, most of them in the US, which specialise in lending to those who have poor financial histories – 'sub-prime', poor-risk borrowers. Once the property market starts to falter, and borrowers fail to keep up their payments, such companies go in for the kill early so as to get the property back at silly money and make a capital gain. As this book goes to press, there are substantial law suits under way in the US where some sub-prime lenders, allegedly, behaved unscrupulously in this way.

Of course not all sub-prime lenders are like this. In the UK, for example, some large, highly-respectable, German and

US banks played an important role in this type of lending. They saw poor-risk borrowers as a legitimate way of extending their market share and, to some extent, took pity on those who couldn't find funds from other sources. After all, if you have a bad credit history or have had county court judgements (CCJs), or even perhaps been repossessed in the past, it can be near-impossible to find someone who'll give you a mortgage. This doesn't make all such borrowers a dead loss for ever, though. Many get back on their feet and, quite reasonably, want to buy a home again at some stage.

Given that a few years from now there'll be millions of people who have fallen foul of the 'borrowing system', there'll be an increased need for sub-prime mortgages. What a paradox!

The UK Government announced, at the beginning of December 2008, measures to help those who are made redundant or whose businesses are failing. In order to prevent the large-scale repossession of homes, the Government will fund a two-year reduction of mortgage interest payments, which will be added to the overall amount borrowed – but repayable by the home owner at a later date.

Under normal circumstances, very few of the 12 million UK existing mortgages in any one year go bad. In 2006 only 17,000 homes were repossessed. In 2007 the figure was 27,000 but in 2008 it looks as if it'll be at least 50,000, so the graph is growing steeply. This growth is occurring because too many people have used their homes as a personal bank and now find that as the cost of living and borrowing rises and the value of their other investments falls, they have over-stretched themselves. Something has to give….and for some, this will be their home.

In the Republic of Ireland, repossession rates are tiny, even allowing for a population that is one fifteenth the size of that of the UK. This very small foreclosure rate is said to be because Irish lenders are closer to their borrowers and take a gentler view on defaulters. In general, British lenders are sensible and understanding but over very recent months they appear to be becoming more unforgiving – with at least one of those bailed out with public funds being draconian.

Hopefully, we won't see the level of foreclosures that the US is currently experiencing. There, one household in every two hundred has been foreclosed upon. Every three months another quarter of a million families lose their homes.

The interest rate danger

The last great UK repossession flood was in the early 1990s when about 75,000 homes a year were taken away from their owners. Some experts today forecast this level of repossessions very soon. Between the start of the recession in 1989 and its end in 1995, more than a third of a million homes had been repossessed. Some of this blood on the streets was caused by exceptionally high interest rates (topping out at fifteen per cent) but even though rates don't come close to this today there are other underlying issues that cause concern, including: rising oil and food prices; the soaring demand for higher living standards in India and China; a highly unstable finance and banking market that threatens even the biggest international banks and corporations not linked to housing; the demands being made by global warming; and the western world's vast level of personal debt. These are just a few of the pressing matters that could influence future interest rates and, thus, housing.

I find that what most shocks people is the increase in their monthly mortgage payments even when the interest rate goes up by a seemingly tiny amount. The reality is that a 0.5% interest rate rise can make a difference of tens or even many hundreds of pounds per month (depending on the size of your mortgage) and a two per cent hike can, over time, be disastrous.

Nobody spells this out to you when offering you a mortgage. I feel strongly that lenders should be legally bound to provide charts of what the repayments would be at every level of interest rate up to, say, twenty per cent. Most people would then try to project what this would mean for the future of their home.

It has become fashionable in recent years to take out fixed-rate mortgages (see page 228). But with this short-term certainty comes the 'reset' issue, when borrowers in huge numbers (about 1.4 million in 2008) come off their fixed rate to be faced with the realities of the true interest rate. This has been called the 'repayment shock'. Trouble is also likely because many people have much larger mortgages than was typical in the '90s. Mortgage borrowings are about double those of the mid-'90s (though most of us aren't earning double), leaving millions of home owners at risk of normal adverse life events such as unemployment, divorce, or illness.

Faced with these negatives, many people now find their home a source of grief. They realise they have over-geared themselves based on its supposed value. Many such families have already taken on more overtime, second jobs and part-time work to increase their borrowing potential. But when interest rates rise and other domestic costs soar, such families are hit hard and their home is under threat, even in an economy with near-full employment and low interest rates. For those with a base-rate tracker mortgage, current low (and falling) interest rates are good news. But for most of us the low rates can't much help as there's so little money around to borrow, however low the interest rate.

In the last spate of repossessions, the government helped by paying the mortgages of those who couldn't keep up. But this system stopped in 1995 on the assumption that most of us would take out mortgage-protection insurance to cover ourselves. However, the majority of us didn't!

Practical options

Even the threat of losing your home can be very stressful. I looked at some of the emotional effects in Chapter Two. A US study found that 38% of those who'd been foreclosed upon felt scared; 35% depressed; 9% angry; and 8% embarrassed. The thing is to be aware of the problems early and to try to do something about them. Most of us tend to deny serious issues until they escalate into something that demands attention...or perhaps the attention of others. But no-one gets repossessed overnight. There are always warning signs, and you can get out of trouble at many stages along the way. Your lender will send you letters asking what's going on and will listen to any reasonable explanation.

The moment you feel at risk (you're falling behind with your payments, for example), get advice from a solicitor or an advice centre. The homeless charity Shelter has an excellent website (www.shelter.org.uk) with a mass of helpful information. A good adviser can start negotiating on your behalf with your lender and could save you nerves, time and money by the whole thing not having to go to court, obviously this will be time and effort well spent.

As I mentioned on page 231, most lenders really do not want to take your home from you. In fact they'll go to considerable lengths not to do so. But to work all this out, you must engage with them and any helpers you enlist because the surest way of going down the tubes is to let things slip or pretend nothing's wrong. Talking can also demonstrate to the court (if you ever get there) that you were trying to sort things out, well before legal action got under way. This always goes down well.

If you can't satisfy your lender that you can pay and they do take you to court (you'll receive a summons), all is not necessarily lost. Most important, for goodness sake turn up. A judge recently said that this was the most important thing anyone can do in this situation. He complained that however helpful he wanted to be, it was always much harder if the borrower didn't show up. A judge can allow you to stay in your home provided you keep to the conditions he lays down; can give you time to sell up to avoid repossession; or can order you out. If it's the last, you'll be given a date by which you'll have to leave. If you do not, then bailiffs can legally evict you.

This said, don't be frightened by lenders' demands that you pay off substantial arrears very quickly. Take advice from people such as the National Debtline; Shelter, and Citizen's Advice Bureau, as they'll have seen it all before. Some county courts also have an advice desk.

Although you may be surprised to hear it, everyone in the whole system will try their very best to enable you to stay in your home. If, for example, you can satisfy the judge that you can clear your arrears before the end of the mortgage period, he could suspend your order for repossession. In 47% of cases this is exactly what happens.

But if the worst comes to the worst and you do lose your home, whether through repossession, or because you've sold it yourself to get out of trouble, what can you do?

Buy another property
In this option you can use any remaining funds you have once your lender and any other debts against your home are paid off to buy somewhere else. This can be tricky if you've had a home repossessed as the new lender will be aware of

your history and may ask for an unusually big deposit and then charge you a higher interest rate. Talk to your council or a local housing advice service about buying a cheaper property through some other sort of scheme in your area.

Rent privately

You could find it hard to get a landlord to take you on as a tenant once you've proven you can't pay your mortgage and have been repossessed. If the landlord can be persuaded that you tried everything you could, or that there were adverse life circumstances you couldn't avoid, then he'll probably take a kindly view but demand a higher deposit up front and insist you always pay your rent in advance. It is unlikely you'll be able to rent social housing or a housing association property unless you've been on their waiting lists. Most such lists are long. For more on this, see page 90.

Get help from your local council

You may be able to be housed temporarily by the council if you are literally homeless. See page 95 for more on this. Talk to an advice centre. If you had a good reason for being unable to pay your mortgage (illness, job loss, divorce, etc) the council will take a more lenient view of your dilemma and may be able to house you somehow. If your council rules that you made yourself intentionally homeless (by not paying your mortgage, for example) they may not be helpful. Seek professional advice before you sell if you intend to approach the council for help afterwards.

Stay with friends or family

This could just be a life-saver. It's unlikely you'll be happy, or even able, to make this a long-term arrangement but it could get you by for some weeks or months. Talk in advance about paying your way. If you've absolutely no resources this won't be possible but it'll be much appreciated if you pay at least something towards your accommodation. It'll also be better for your dignity, as you won't feel such a 'charity case'.

Other possibilities

As a very last resort you could look at living in supported housing or living in a housing co-op. Contact a local housing aid centre, Citizen's Advice Bureau, or other advice centre.

For some people, being repossessed is a serious nuisance but not the end of their world. If life has dealt them a blow they can often rent for a while, get back on their feet and even own a home again, one day.

However, for some, the loss of their home is just the tip of a much bigger financial iceberg. If the money from selling your home doesn't cover your debts, this can be a serious problem. If you had a mortgage indemnity guarantee from an insurance company this will pay off your lender but your lender can still take action against you for the main part of your outstanding loan. Get independent advice at once if you have such a policy. An adviser will also be able to tell you how you'll be able to pay back any debts. Your lender could write off part of your debt; agree for you to pay a reduced lump sum as a final settlement; or arrange for you to pay things off over an agreed timescale. Or you could declare yourself bankrupt. This last option might, at first, seem appealing but take advice because it could seriously affect your future.

A useful website if you have debt problems is www.nationaldebtline.co.uk They also have an advice line number: 0808 808 4000.

Chapter 10
SIXTEEN LESSONS FROM PREVIOUS CRASHES

As a property developer friend replied when I asked him what we could learn from the '90s crash: 'We obviously learned nothing at all!'

This said, certain patterns become apparent when trying to discover how we got here. Whether any insights discerned over the last forty years will help prevent it happening again is quite another matter. All I can say is, I wish someone had told me these things when I was twenty!

LESSON 1
The property market is not homogeneous. The 'market' is, in reality, a mass of tiny sub-markets. Even within one small town there may be several sub-markets – all differing from one another. In a big city, these differences can be huge so don't be seduced into even thinking of 'the property market' as a single entity behaving in a particular way. The press and other media tend to do this but it's simplistic, creates erroneous impressions, worries people unnecessarily, and can mask the truth.

LESSON 2

When the market 'cools' it takes a long time to turn completely into 'ice'. In other words, it's always possible, given some care and insight, to be aware of what's happening long before disaster strikes. Only overly-optimistic or foolish people refuse to see the writing on the wall. There is usually enough time to get out or to re-think your housing before things get desperate. Don't go into denial. When things start looking tricky, don't go the headless-chicken route. Instead, act speedily if you intend to, or need to.

LESSON 3

Keep an eye on employment in your area. This affects prices for both good and bad.

LESSON 4

Don't over-stretch yourself financially unless you are completely relaxed about losing your home! Borrow less than you can. Or even choose not to borrow at all, if you possibly can. Remember that half of all home-owners in Britain have no mortgage. Even if this means lowering your sights, you'll never regret it. I know this may seem heretical in a property-obsessed culture but it's true. In reality, more than a million British households have enough spare cash or savings to keep them going for only two weeks if they were to lose their job!

LESSON 5

Remember that every time we overpay for a house and gear ourselves up to the hilt, it makes the market spin that little bit faster for everyone else. If you have children who are trying to get a home, you'll know exactly what this means. The greed and stupidity of the baby-boomer generation has created a property hell for our kids. We have a lot to answer for. Some parents are helping their youngsters get into the market, be it out of goodwill, love or guilt; but many are not – or cannot. Some are spending their property windfalls on other things while their children look on, wondering how they will cope.

LESSON 6

Your home is not a bank. Just because for a few years it has appeared to be one doesn't mean this will continue. Take out a mortgage you can easily afford to repay even if things go wrong...and then pretend you're paying a rent. Millions of people in other countries pay rent every month and never think of their homes as piggybanks. Investing in a personal bank like this is fallacious in all but an exceptional market...and who'd run their life governed by exceptions?

LESSON 7

Don't think of landlords as rogues or social pariahs. Rental housing is going to become a commonplace feature of the UK property market of the future. Relax into this and see if it might suit you better than buying. There's no shame in it. Perhaps rent your main home and buy a small holiday home, as millions of Continentals do. Or do other non-property-related things to add to your quality of life.

LESSON 8

Try to build up a savings kitty of enough money to keep you afloat for a half a year, should you lose your job, get divorced, or become seriously ill.

LESSON 9

Watch out for new building and developments. In general, developers do their research before risking their money. Ride on the back of their decisions. I know this might seem bad advice at this particular moment (when builders and developers are suffering from circumstances outside their control) but over time it tends to be true.

LESSON 10

Booms always end in busts, stagnation or corrections. There has never been a time since World War II that a property boom hasn't been adjusted somehow. Don't be surprised when this happens....it's inevitable, given human nature and the way we currently run our property market.

LESSON 11

Once something adverse happens in the housing market, it takes far longer than you'd think to get back to its previous state. Think years, rather than months.

LESSON 12

When trying to read the market, be aware that investors are cannier than you and have more to lose. This means that they get out, or in, faster than normal home buyers. If you want to keep ahead of the game, watch what they do.

LESSON 13

Never over-extend yourself in a poor market. A bargain is never a bargain if you can't afford it.

LESSON 14

Try at all times not to lose sight of common sense. Rely on your instinct rather than what the pundits, the media, the finance industry or estate agents tell you. Bear in mind that by the time you read something in a daily paper, the pros have already been there and done that!

LESSON 15

A downturn in the economy and a slowing of house prices need not be all bad. This could be a great time to slow down in general, to take stock of your finances, and even how you run your life as a whole. There's little point making a drama out of a crisis. Try to remember that the Chinese word for crisis is 'danger-opportunity'.

LESSON 16

If something seems to be too good to be true in the world of property…rest assured it probably is!

ACKNOWLEDGEMENTS

I would like to thank the following people who helped me with specific areas of the book:

Mortgages: Minesh Patel of EA Financial Solutions

Social Housing: Martyn Kingsford

Large-scale property development: Alan Chorlton

I would also like to thank Jeremy Leaf, a North London chartered surveyor and estate agent, who kindly read through parts of the manuscript.

INDEX